YOUR PARENTS WILL SLEEP BETTER AT NIGHT: THE COMPLETE EDUCATION MANUAL FOR NEW DRIVERS

WITH 3 TIPS THAT YOU WOULD NEVER THINK OF

ZACH ALEXANDER

BOOK DESCRIPTION

Learning to drive is one of the most exciting times of your life. It's probably the first of many milestones you will have in your life that turn you from a child into an adult. It's a pretty big deal, and I'm here to help guide you through it in a fun and informative way. As we've heard many times before, "with great power comes great responsibility."

In this book we will move through all the phases that start with you studying for your learner's license test, all the way to what you should do in case of an accident. I will help you define what kind of driver you should be and the steps you need to get there.

I want you to feel confident, excited, calm and in control when you get behind that wheel. I also want your parents to feel the same way. I approach my driving wisdom through the eyes of a parent that has taught two teens how to drive. I also have driven all over the world and draw on my own mistakes and experience to ensure you will be a safer driver with great common sense that your parents will never worry about.

indirect, that are incurred due to the use of the information in this document, including, but not limited to, errors, omissions, or inaccuracies.

CONTENTS

"The one thing that unites all human beings, regardless of age, gender, religion, economic status, or ethnic background, is that, deep down inside, we all believe that we are above-average drivers."

— DAVE BARRY

INTRODUCTION

When I was fourteen, I came home from school to find my dad hanging up the phone and laughing uncontrollably. This was a rarity for him so I was very curious to know what his conversation was about. His friend Jerry had called to tell him about his son Michael's driving test. It turns out that Michael had passed his driver's test with flying colors. What on earth could have happened that caused my dad to laugh so hard about someone passing their driver's test?

That morning Jerry took Michael to take his driver's license test at the Department of Motor Vehicles (DMV). They had practiced so much that Jerry didn't even stick around to make sure he passed. He had Michael's mom pick him up because surely he would be able to drive himself home afterwards. Michael had done everything right. He got a perfect score. The tester even said it was some of the best parallel parking he had ever seen.

Michael was thrilled and excitedly went into the building to get his photo taken and finish up the paperwork. He thanked everyone in the room, did a little victory dance, and raced out the front door to take his first solo drive as a new driver. This was a big moment. He turned the car on, threw it in reverse, and backed right over the curb, crushed the flowers, and smashed through the plate glass window of the DMV building. Thankfully no one was hurt, and a potentially terrifying situation became a funny and expensive story. Michael did not drive for another 2 years after this incident, and he has been the target of many jokes for decades.

Although entertaining to envision, his story is a cautionary one. No matter how prepared someone might think that they are to be a driver, things can go sideways very quickly. Being a great driver is a combination of knowledge, practical skills, common sense, emotional calmness and awareness. Michael had knowledge, practical skills, and a bit of common sense, but he let his emotions and awareness slip and he paid the price.

Getting your driver's license is a big responsibility but probably one of the most exciting moments of your life. It's a big milestone that opens up new possibilities. You will have a sense of freedom that you have never experienced before, and that is really thrilling. I remember very vividly that first moment that I sat behind the wheel all by myself. I felt so cool, like I had joined a new club. I would find all sorts of reasons to drive places. I became the official errand runner for my parents. To put it bluntly, driving is awesome.

As a driver, I have decades of experience all over the world and in every type of situation you can imagine. Growing up, my parents owned a grocery store, and I worked there from a young age. Every week we had trucks deliver inventory, and I loved hearing about their traveling stories as they transported goods all across the country. It sparked that feeling in me that driving is equal to freedom and adventure. When I became a young adult, I embarked on many road trips around the world which gave me invaluable experience to be comfortable in all driving situations.

As a parent I have successfully taught two confident teenage-driver's that I trust completely. I have used my unique level of driving experience to help them, and this is what I will use to help you. I know what it takes to be a great driver, and be comfortable as a parent having my loved ones out on the road by themselves. When you are done reading this book, you will be equipped to handle all sorts of situations and show your parents that you are a reliable and safe driver.

My goal with this book is to make you a confident driver with everything you need to enjoy operating a vehicle safely. If you have any reservations about your ability to drive or your parents are worried about letting you off on your own, we will solve them together and with the help of our friend Alex who you will meet momentarily. On the flip side of that, if you think you are the best driver in the world and you don't feel like you need much help, I can make you aware of things that you might not think of to get you out there safely. We will go over everything from the basics of driving, vehicle knowledge, driving scenarios, tips to practice, and more. Let's get started on this fun experience together.

1

STEPS TO GETTING YOUR LICENSE

"If you don't know where you are going, any road will get you there."

— LEWIS CARROL

I'd like to introduce you to Alex. As we progress through the book, Alex will help demonstrate and educate you about various tips and situations to be a great driver. With Alex we will give you the knowledge you need to be the best driver you can be. With the same sentiment as the quote above, he will help teach you the points that you didn't even know you needed to know.

You are finally old enough to take your driver's test. How do you feel about it? You might have been counting down the days for the last year, or maybe you haven't given it much thought. I'm guessing if you are reading this, it's because you are thinking about going for it and you might have some reservations. That's normal and totally fine. Everybody has a little bit of apprehension when going for their driver's test.

The good news is that you are working on your own timeline and there is no rush or deadline to get your license at any particular time. Take as much time as you need to feel comfortable. Even after you pass your license, you can continue to practice with trusted driver's until you are ready to go out on your own.

LEARNER'S LICENSE FIRST

The first question is where do you start? What is the first step to getting your license? Before getting your full driver's license, you will take a written test to get your learner's license. A learner's license is a stepping stone where you have demonstrated enough knowledge about road safety to operate a vehicle under the supervision of another driver, but you aren't ready to do it on your own just yet.

In preparation for taking your learner's test, you can pick up a driver's manual from your local DMV. Most states also have the most recent copy available online as well. The test is going to focus on understanding road signs and basic road rules. Read the manual thoroughly and do practice quizzes with friends or family. There is a cost to taking the written learner's test, so you want to pass it on your first try to save yourself paying more than once. The cost varies from state to state but usually falls around $100.

In preparation for taking his learner's test, Alex designed a study schedule for himself. He picked a date that he would like to take his test and then broke down the amount of material he needed to cover by day. He figured out that he needed to study for 30 min 5 days a week to get everything accomplished.

In some select states, you may need to take a driver's education course to qualify to take the learner's test as well. Take a look at the requirements of your state online or by going into a DMV. The last thing you want is to study really hard and get excited only to find out that you can't book your test until you have completed additional requirements. Specific requirements that you will want to look into include:

- What age do you need to be to take your learner's test? It ranges between 14-16 years of age minimum.
- How much does it cost?

- Do you require a driver's education course to take either the learner's or driver's tests?
- What languages is the test offered in? If English is not your first language, you may have the option to study and take the test in your preferred language.
- If you don't pass the test the first time (which no worries you will with all your studying), is there a time period you have to wait until you take the next one?
- Do you need an appointment, or can you just walk in?

Remember to take your glasses or contacts with you when you are taking the test for your learner's permit. You will be required to take an eye exam prior to them issuing your license.

If your learner's or full driver's license states that you require glasses and you are not wearing them if you are pulled over, or if you are in an accident then you will be ticketed or found at fault. Always remember to wear your glasses while driving if required.

Don't stress about taking the written test for your learner's. You will pass it as long as you read the driver's manual and take your time studying. Many signs you will be familiar with just being a passenger over the years. There are many rules to the road that you may not have been aware of, but they will become second nature with time. If you take your time and learn the driver's manual thoroughly you will have no problems at all.

Parent Tip: When my oldest daughter was old enough to take her learner's license, she took it upon herself to get all the information she needed to take her test. She called the DMV to ask all the questions and found out their business hours, so I could drive her down there to get a manual. She then made herself a study schedule where she studied for 30 min every night until she was very comfortable with the material. At this point, she asked me to quiz her on her knowledge. Her maturity and dedication to learning the process and the material was very impressive to me. It was the first step towards me feeling very comfortable at how seriously she was taking it. If you take this same approach, I guarantee your parents will be happy with your attitude and more willing to help you practice driving once you are able to.

LEARNING TO DRIVE

It's happening! You have your learner's license, and you are now officially legal to get behind the wheel. Congratulations! First things first, here are a few basic questions you are going to want to ask before you leave the DMV with your brand new Learner's permit:

- How long is it valid for?
- Is there a minimum number of months you need to have your learner's license before taking your driver's test?
- Do you need to log a certain number of hours with your learner's before applying for your driver's test?
- Is it required for you to take a driver's education course?

- Is there a course offered through your high school?
- If you have to take a private driver's education course, how much is the cost?
- How far in advance do you need to book your driver's test appointment?
- Will they provide a vehicle, or do you need to come with your own?

Whether you are required to take a driver's education course or not, if it's in the budget, I highly recommend it. I ended up having to take two separate courses because I didn't do my research and took a privately offered one that wasn't certified and had to take a second one to be eligible for my driver's test. Although it was disheartening at the time, I did get a lot of extra practice and learned things from both instructors. Important note here to make sure that you are enrolling in the correct course if it is required by your state. Learn from my silly error.

If you are not going to take a driver's course, there are many resources online as to what you will need to know for your state. Make sure to talk to someone at your local DMV to see what resources they offer.

Parent Tip: Finding out information about driver's education and presenting it to your parents will once again instill confidence that you are taking this very seriously. If there is a cost associated with lessons, offer to chip in to pay, or do extra work around the house to earn them. If you will not be taking lessons, coming up with a lesson plan they can follow with you and a schedule will really impress them. Also it will be beneficial to you to have a plan in place to make sure you learn everything you need to know.

The Driver's Ed Guru offers a free online driver's plan that acts as a general guide to lessons you will need to follow. Below is a summary of the great advice he offers ("Know Someone Learning to Drive? We're Here to Help!"). He breaks up your learning into four stages:

1. Stage 1: The Empty Parking Lot: Getting familiar with driving. Approximate duration of practice time 2-4 weeks
2. Stage 2: Low Risk Streets: Venturing out into non busy areas to practice basic driving skills. Approximate duration of practice time 2-5 weeks
3. Stage 3: High Volume Streets: Moving into busier city streets with lots of traffic. Approximate duration of practice time 2-5 weeks
4. Stage 4: Highway driving and Hazardous conditions: Learning the differences to driving

on highways and through bad weather. Approximate duration of practice time depends on time of year for weather and accessibility to highways.

The full details of driving education are a manual all on their own. I could write a hundred pages in detail of all the lessons you need to go over all the aspects of driving responsibility. Since we have a lot of other topics to go over, and there are many resources online as well as your parents' experience, I will provide a list of all the skills you should master before taking your test, as well as a few examples of lessons I learned through my own training:

List of driving skills you should be comfortable with before taking your test:

- Parking - straight, angled and parallel
- Smooth Pedal operation
- Turning
- Lane Changing
- Reversing
- Braking in all situations
- Driving different sizes and types of cars
- parking lot knowledge
- emergency braking

- spatial awareness with other vehicles and objects
- Two point turns, three point turns and U-turns
- Road awareness and scanning
- following directions and finding locations through maps and guided navigation
- Intersections
- Roundabouts
- Merging
- Night Driving
- Highway driving
- Passing on two lane highways
- Handling skidding
- What to do when you lose control of the vehicle due to ice, rain, or gravel
- Emergency situations
- Driving in hazardous conditions

Take this list and do additional research to add in any other lessons you find applicable. For example, if you live in a city with a lot of roundabouts you may want a lesson completely on this topic for one day.

Parent Tip: Make yourself a practice and training schedule that your parents can look over before you start. It will show them that you have a good understanding of what you need to learn and

Day one behind the wheel is a big one. If you have never driven a car before it is going to be exciting, daunting, and uncomfortable all at once. Have your parents drive you to an empty parking lot to start your training. Schools on weekends and evenings are usually quite vacant, or mall parking lots on Sunday evenings are empty if they close early.

The first thing you do is familiarize yourself with your surroundings before you even get in.

Step 1: Take a walk around the car. Look at your tires to make sure one is not visible lower than the others. Look at the ground to check for nails, broken glass, or other debris. Take notice of people or objects in your vicinity. Once you are in the vehicle, there are certain things you can't see so taking note of them now is extremely important.

To demonstrate the importance of checking around the vehicle, one of my driving instructors had a little trick. On the second or third lesson after I had been taught to check our surroundings, he stopped reminding me and just got in the vehicle as we were chatting and walking towards it. I followed his lead and just hopped right in.

We then went through all of the steps before starting the vehicle (which we will go over shortly), and he asked me to slowly back up. Next I heard a loud crunching sound and my stomach flipped. I momentarily panicked before slamming my foot on the break. The instructor calmly asked me to put it into park and turn the vehicle off. He then asked me to step out of the vehicle and survey the damage. At this point I was almost ready to turn and run and never look back. Much to my relief, I came around the back of the car to see two sheets of bubble wrap under the wheels. The instructor then explained that it only takes once for that bubble wrap to be a person to change a life, or something sharp and dangerous to damage my vehicle. It was a lesson I never forgot. I can still hear that sound and feel my panic as to what I might have done. Those areas that you can't see once you are in the vehicle are deceivingly large. In addition I mentioned for you to take note of people in the areas. If there are children playing it only takes a moment for them to run after a ball and behind your car while you are getting ready inside. Make sure you are aware of where they are before you start moving the vehicle.

Step 2: Once you are fully aware of the outside of the vehicle, get on in. Before you do anything, put your seatbelt on and put your phone away. Those will be the two biggest habits any parent wants to see their child do. Repeat it a few times to yourself. Seatbelt on, phone away. Seatbelt on, phone away. When I say phone away, I don't mean in a cup holder or within reach, I mean tucked away in a bag, the glove compartment, or placed in the backseat.

Parent Tip: For many of us parents, cell phones weren't quite in existence yet when we started driving. Certainly not to the extent that they are used by teens now. I think every parent's biggest fear when their kids start driving in today's world is that they will be distracted by their phones. It's a bigger risk factor now than drinking and driving because pretty much every single teen has a phone. If the first time you get into the car with a parent and they see that you are forming the habit of seatbelt on, phone away, their anxiety level will drop immensely.

Step 3: Now you will adjust your mirrors and seat. You have your rearview mirror and your side mirrors. These are your eyes to the surroundings of the car while driving. Make sure to adjust them that you can see very clearly along both sides of the vehicle and behind you. Next adjust your seat so that you can comfortably press the pedals, but not too close that your arms are tucked in too tight. Make sure that your arms are slightly bent. Place your hands at "10 and 2" on the steering wheel. If you think of your steering wheel as a clock, put your left hand where the 10 would be and your right hand where the 2 would be. This is the placement that gives you the most control over the vehicle and the ability to react quickly in case of an emergency.

Step 4: When you are all ready and set, turn the vehicle on. That's it! Lesson 1. It might sound very simple, but they are all very important steps to set you up for safe driving.

For each one of your lessons, take the time to map out a clear plan for your parents to help you with. Use lessons plans you find online as a guide to creating a thorough driving practice plan.

Alex is explaining to his son that being patient and thorough is the key to success in obtaining your driver's license. There is no rush, and that he will be a great driver by studying and practicing. Keep open communication with your parents about where you are at with your comfort level through the training process. If you get stuck on something and don't feel fully confident, ask them to practice that skill with you until you do.

2

GETTING FAMILIAR WITH THE PARTS OF YOUR VEHICLE

"Show Me Your Car and I'll Tell You Who You Are."

Successfully obtaining your driver's license is the beginning of a whole new exciting time in your life. By now you are comfortable with the rules of the road, and how to confidently operate an automobile. The next thing you are going to want to know is about the car itself. I am not asking you to become a certified mechanic by any means. I just want you to be comfortable with some general knowledge of your vehicle.

A simple way to look at this is your knowledge of the human body and your overall medical background. You have enough knowledge to know how things look and feel about yourself, so if something is wrong, you can identify it and get yourself to a doctor. The same goes for your vehicle, you don't need to know how to fix the car, you just need to be able to identify when you should take it to a mechanic. As well, there are simple things that you can do yourself. If you get a cut, you don't go to the doctor, you clean it and put a Band-Aid on. The same for your vehicle, if you need to replace the wipers, or do simple replacements, you can perform these yourself and save money in the process.

There are two other ways that we can compare your body to your car. First, you have to take care of our car like you do your body. If you don't feed your body with proper nutrition, do annual health check ups, and get regular exercise, you will eventually get sick and not feel as well. The same goes for your car, you need to do regular maintenance, treat it property, and get regular check ups to make sure there are no issues.

The second way to look at it is proper cleanliness. You like to take care of your hygiene and look good because it says a lot about you as a person. Treat your car the same way. Keep it clean and tidy. Having loose items and garbage around your vehicle not only looks messy but it can be unsafe as well.

10 ITEMS YOU SHOULD HAVE IN YOUR VEHICLE AT ALL TIMES

Within your vehicle there are a variety of items and things that you should be able to locate within minutes. Familiarizing yourself with these things is very important.

The first three items are your License, insurance, and registration.

1. Never leave home without your license. If you are pulled over, the officer will give you a ticket for operating a vehicle without a license. Always remember to check to see if you have it.

2. Once you have your license and you start driving, your vehicle must be insured. Whether it's your own vehicle, or you are borrowing your parents, your insurance must be up to date. Usually it is located in the glovebox. If you will be using your parents' vehicle, make sure that their insurance covers additional driver's other than themselves.

3. In addition to insurance, your vehicle must be registered. Your local registry where you went to get your license is also where you register your vehicle. The purpose of registering your vehicle is that the state knows you exist and that you are out there on the road. It shows that your vehicle belongs to you, and also helps in case of an accident or missing vehicle.

Parent Tip: Don't make it your parent's responsibility to acquire insurance and registration for you. Find out what you need to drive their vehicle or your own, and make it your own actions to get it taken care of.

Next there are various items in the vehicle that you may need for various emergency situations. If your vehicle does not have these items in them, make sure to get them to have them on hand.

1. First Aid Kit - You never know what situation that might come up where you need access to a first aid kit. My cousin was once in an accident during a snowstorm and was stranded in a snow covered ditch. (I will go over some additional snow safety items shortly in case that is your climate). He cut his hand quite badly and did not have a first aid kit to clean the wound or bandage it up. He wrapped a piece of clothing around it temporarily but it would have been way better and safer if he had his kit with him.

2. Fire Extinguisher - It is a rare event that you would ever need a fire extinguisher, but you definitely want it just in case.

3. Inflated Spare Tire - Getting a flat tire stinks. It's even worse if you don't have a ready to swap out inflated spare tire. Make sure yours is always ready. If you need to use your spare time, make sure to check it over before you put it back once you get a replacement tire or your old one fixed.

4. A Jack - Many vehicles come with a Jack. A jack is an apparatus used to prop your vehicle up high enough that you can get the old tire off in case of a flat tire and replace it with the spare.

You absolutely need one in case of a flat tire. If your vehicle doesn't come with one, make sure to buy one.

5. Jumper Cables - Sometimes your vehicle's battery may die for a variety of reasons. Maybe you accidently left a light on, or the weather is too cold and its having trouble starting. Jumper cables will enable you to get a boost from another vehicle. They are also helpful to have on hand in case someone needs a boost from you.

6. A Flashlight - If you ever break down on the side of the road in the evening, or if you are in a situation where you need light and it's at nighttime, you will definitely be happy that you packed a flashlight. Every few months make sure to check and see that it still works and that it hasn't run out of batteries.

7. Winter Pack - When you live in a climate with snow and ice there are some additional items you will want on hand in your vehicle.

8. Chains for your tires - in very slippery and icy road conditions, chains can provide traction and prevent you from slipping off the road.

9. Sand or Cat Litter - You may be wondering why on earth you would need these items. In

icy conditions you may get your vehicle stuck where your tired spin and can't get enough grip to propel the vehicle forward. Spreading either cat Litter or sand around the tired can enable them to get enough grip to move out of the place that you are stuck in.

10. Warm clothing - Every time you get into a vehicle in winter, even if you aren't dressed to spend time outside, always make sure you have full winter gear and blankets for everyone in the car. If you get a flat tire and need time to change it, you want to make sure you have proper clothing and that any people waiting inside the car are also warm.

11. Candles - a candle can provide warmth in an emergency situation. The cousin that I mentioned earlier went into a ditch and the vehicle was half covered with snow. **When the exhaust pipe of the vehicle is covered in snow, you cannot turn the vehicle on for warmth**. This is a deadly situation. The vehicle will fill with carbon monoxide and the situation will be fatal. He was able to stay warm by using a small candle for warmth until someone came by to help him. He was in the ditch for hours waiting for a vehicle to drive by and he didn't

have warm enough clothing on so he said it might have saved his life.

Making sure you have the proper items in your car can be life saving in certain situations. Also make sure they are packed away neatly and you are familiar with all their locations so that when you need items you don't waste valuable time looking for them during an emergency.

Parent Tip: Knowing that your child is prepared in their vehicle and that being prepared is priority to you makes a parent feel extremely safe.

PARTS OF THE CAR YOU WILL WANT TO KNOW

Now that we know what contents should be in your car, it's time to learn terminology of vehicle parts and some terms you will find handy.

Pop Quiz!

How many of the following car parts are you familiar with?

- ABS
- filters
- Chassis

- PSI
- Fuel injection
- Engine combustion

If you are like most people, you probably aren't familiar with many of them. That's what I'm here for. To help you understand what each of these are and why you want to know a little bit about them.

ABS - Anti-Lock Braking System

Almost all vehicles in the last decade now have ABS as a standard feature. What this system does is pump the brakes very rapidly when it senses that your wheels are locking up to help keep control of the vehicle. You keep your foot firmly on the brake, and the system will pump rapidly to help gain traction and maintain control of the vehicle. ("Anti-Lock Braking System: MyCarDoesWhat.org"). Maintaining the components of your brake system, and keeping your tires inflated will ensure that your ABS works properly and keeps you safe.

When your ABS light comes on there are four possible reasons ("Four Reasons Your ABS Light Is On"):

1. Something is wrong with your ABS module - This will need to be diagnosed by a mechanic.
2. Low Brake fluid - All braking systems need brake fluid. You may have low fluid levels which can cause the light to come on.
3. Wheel sensors are broken - The way your ABS knows what your tires are doing to ensure it is correct their traction is through sensors. If one of these sensors are broken or dirty it can cause too much information to be sent to the system so it recognizes that something is not working properly, and the ABS light comes on. Before taking your vehicle in, clean the tires and restart the vehicle to see if the light goes off.
4. You turned it off - most vehicles have the ability to turn the ABS off. It can help in certain situations like if you are trying to get out of a slippery rut. However, the majority of the time you are best to keep your ABS on. So you may have accidentally bumped the button to turn it off without realizing it. Try turning them back

on and then turn your vehicle off and restart it to see if the light goes out.

Filters

There are 3 filters that will need replacing annually or usually every 12000 miles depending on your vehicle. Each type of filter has a purpose and is necessary to your vehicle running properly. Depending on the make and model of your vehicle, you can probably change most of the filters on your own which can save you a lot of money rather than having it done by a mechanic. ("FAQs about Your Car's Fuel and Air Filters | Firestone Complete Auto Care")

1. Air Filter - The air filter protects your engine from dust and debris on the road. When you don't change your air filter, you will notice

lower fuel economy and it can result in higher emissions. Even your ability to accelerate quickly can be lower when you have a very clogged air filter. That's a big deal!

2. Cabin Filter - This filter is to keep your breathing air clean and dust free. Whether you're driving in the city or in the country, there are a variety of contaminants and other items that you want to keep out of your lungs so having a clean cabin filter is ideal. When it is very dirty, you will notice a difference in your cabin air quality usually by smell.

3. Fuel Filter - Your fuel filter keeps your fuel lines clean by filtering out any dust, dirt and debris that can get into your fuel tank. If your fuel filter gets really dirty it can actually cause a cut off of fuel to the fuel lines and cause your vehicle to think it's out of gas and stop. That is the worst case scenario and can absolutely be avoided. If you notice a big difference in your fuel efficiency this can be a sign that it's time to change the filter.

Making yourself a schedule for changing your filters and sticking to it can prevent any issues that come from lack of maintenance. Also by knowing when your filters need to be changed and familiar with their maintenance can prevent you from being taken advantage of.

I remember a family friend telling me that she was so angry because she went to get her oil changed, and the business told her that she desperately needed a cabin filter change. She insisted that she had just changed it and that it was fine. They told her that she put it in incorrectly and that she would do damage to the vehicle if she didn't put the proper size in. Doubting her skills, she agreed and paid for the new filter but asked to keep the old one. She then went back to the parts store where she had bought it and asked them to come look at the difference in the one that they installed and they told her it was the exact same filter. She was so upset she went right back to the oil change business and confronted them. She was so upset with herself too that she doubted her knowledge. If you know your filters, plus when and how they need to be changed you can take control of your own vehicle maintenance needs.

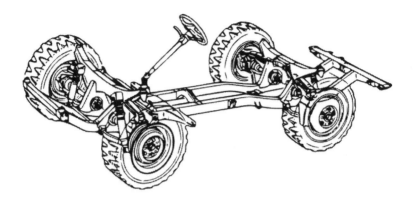

Chassis

Your vehicle's chassis is the frame and support for the entire vehicle. It's kind of like your skeleton. Everything is built around and on it. You need a strong base to support all the components of the vehicle. It is also responsible for how your vehicle handles, towing capabilities, and how your vehicle will react during an accident.

What's important to know about your chassis is how to protect it. For example, if you don't have a chassis that is meant for offroading in a field, and you put your vehicle through trying to do something funny, you could end up with a pretty big bill to fix it. Another situation would be if you tried to tow something really heavy with a vehicle that has a low towing capability you could damage the frame as well.

If you ever question whether or not you may have damaged your frame by being in an accident or doing something with your vehicle that you shouldn't have, get it checked by a certified mechanic before continuing to drive your vehicle.

PSI - Pounds Per Square Inch

Your tire pressure is measured in PSI. To check your pressure, you use a pressure gauge. These can be found at the gas station, auto repair shop, or you can buy one for home. In your driver's manual, it will tell you the ideal PSI for your vehicles. Quite often the information can be found on a sticker along the edge of your car door as well.

On each tire you have a stem with a valve cover. You screw the cover off and press the gauge up against the valve stem. The gauge will have a numbered line pop out the bottom and will stop at the numerical value of your PSI. If you are in the correct range for your vehicle that's great! If you are underinflated, you use an air compressor to inflate. If you are over inflated, you can press the valve to the side and listen for the hissing of air coming out. Keep checking as you add or remove air to get it into the right range.

Some things to know about tire pressure ("6 Things You Need to Know about Tire Pressure"):

1. Weather can affect your tire pressure. If you live in a climate with harsh winters, as the temperature drops, so does your tire pressure. When the seasons change you may have to check the pressure and adjust.

2. An Overinflated tire is bad. An over inflated tire provides less contact points with the road and your tire. For this reason, it gives you less control of the vehicle. It also creates uneven wear and the tires and can cause them to wear out quicker than average.

3. An Underinflated tire is also bad. It can provide too much contact with the road which is prone to hydroplaning. Hydroplaning is when a layer of water separates the tire from the road and you don't have any traction or grip so you

vehicle skids along the layer of water with no ability to grip the road and stop. An underinflated tire also decreases fuel efficiency, which is an expensive problem for you!

Fuel Injection

Your fuel injection system controls the amount of fuel being put into the engine to keep your car running smoothly. When the system breaks down, so does your car's ability to operate properly.

Most often the check engine light will come if you are having an issue with your fuel injection system. Other symptoms can include, rough idling, poor gas mileage, your vehicle won't start, or it misfires.

Usually it's dirt and debris that are clogging the fuel injection system to work improperly. The first option to try and fix the problem is a fuel injector cleaner kit from an auto parts shop. This is much less expensive than heading to the dealership right away. However, if you try the kit, and the problem does not seem fixed, you may have to turn to a professional to help you source and fix the problem.

Engine Combustion

When it comes to your vehicle's engine, there is no need for an in depth explanation of how it operates.

And to be honest, I couldn't give you one anyway. Not many drivers know the ins and outs of how an engine operates. You don't necessarily need to know how it works, you just need to know how to take care of it and recognize when things aren't running correctly.

Here are a few things that you should know about your engine and its performance (Liquori):

1. The lifetime of your engine - There is a certain amount of consistency of how long an engine will last, but even with all the same factors, some engines last longer than others. By providing good maintenance and driving responsibly, you can expect to get at least 100,00 miles, and more likely closer to 200,000.

2. How do you know when your engine is in trouble? - When your car shakes, makes weird

noises, smokes, or leaks, it's time to get it to a mechanic. When you check engine light comes on and is flashing as opposed to on solidly, that is an indicator that you should take it into a repair shop right away.

3. Why is maintenance important? - It's plain and simple. Maintenance will prolong the lifetime of your engine and save you money in the long run. Using fuel additives and engine flushes to remove dirt, debris, and contaminants can help the health of the individual parts of the engine and the long term performance.

The bottom line is that if you lift the hood of your car and it looks like an alien planet in there, that's ok. By no means do you need to know how to build an engine, inspect your chassis, or change your brake pads. To be safe on the road, all you need to know is how to identify problems as they arise, and small maintenance checks such as tire pressure regularly to keep you safe.

Parent Tip: Owning and maintaining a car is not cheap. Regular maintenance, tire replacements, and unforeseen problems can add up quickly. Try to plan ahead and put aside a repair fund rather than waiting for things to come up and needing to ask for money or dipping into credit. Showing responsibility by thinking ahead shows a lot of maturity.

CAR LANGUAGE

After years of driving, certain terminology becomes second nature. As a new driver, you might hear words or phrases that you've never encountered before. To avoid looking like a newbie or unknowledgeable, I would like to help you out.

Handling - Refers to how a vehicle responds when it turns. When a vehicle turns with a thigh radius, parks great, and drives very easily, you will hear people say, "It handles well".

Jump Start - This refers to when your car battery dies and it needs a jolt of electricity to get it started again. You can get a jump start by using special cables called "jumper cables" that connect your car battery to another vehicle's battery.

Drivability - Most simply put, it's your car's ability to drive. The smoother, faster, and nicer the acceleration and ability to slow down, the better the drivability of a vehicle.

RPM - Revolutions or rotations per minute. It refers to how quickly the rotation of the crank delivers power to the engine.

WOT - Wide open throttle. Fully open up the engine. Basically put the metal to the metal.

Hard stops - Opposed to delicately tapping the brake pedal, or slowly easing to a slower pace, you slam on the brakes to react to something unexpected. Hard stops are very hard on your vehicle but are necessary sometimes.

Towing - When your vehicle is inoperable and needs to be pulled by a tow truck to a repair shop.

3

TAKING CARE OF YOUR VEHICLE

"Take Care of your car in the garage, and the car will take care of you on the road"

— AMIT KALANTRI

Every car has its own needs for maintenance. An older vehicle is going to need more, and a new vehicle will need less in the beginning. It's your responsibility as a driver to keep your car in good condition so it's safe for you, your passengers, and other drivers on the road.

You might think to yourself, how does it affect anyone else if my vehicle is working or not? I'm the one that will have to pay the bill, or get stuck on the side of the road. Let me give you a few scenarios to demonstrate my point.

In the first scenario, your tires are underinflated. You noticed a few days ago, but haven't had time to check the tire pressure and get to a gas station to put some air in them. On your way home from school it starts pouring out. As we discussed earlier, underinflated tires make you prone to hydroplaning. On a busy road, you lose control of your vehicle and crash directly into the vehicle next to you. In the process, you both end up stopped after you bump into a bus stop. **Luckily,** you were not traveling at high speeds, and no one was at the bus stop, so the cars are damaged but everyone is ok. The situation could have been much worse, and you still have a big headache of repairs and increased insurance on your hands. Now you think back and wish you had taken the 10 minutes to stop and put air in your tires. Procrastinating maintenance can have big consequences.

In the second scenario, you don't do regular checks of your lights to make sure they are all working correctly. You come to a four way stop and think you have your left turn signal light on, but the front bulb is burnt out. The car facing you assumes that you will go straight because they can't see your front turn signal blinking and when you turn, they don't have enough time to react and you run right into each other. Again you are lucky that your speed was low, but you have an expensive mistake on your hands, and a very angry driver to deal with.

In both of these fictional scenarios, no one was hurt. However, in real life, an accident caused by a poorly maintained vehicle can result in dire consequences such as fatality. So maintenance is not to be taken lightly.

Now that you understand the importance of taking care of your car, let's get into the proper way to do it so you don't ever have to worry that your car isn't in tip top shape.

GET FAMILIAR WITH YOUR CAR

I will be completely honest, I don't think I've ever pulled out a manual from the glove compartment and read the entire thing cover to cover. There's a lot of information in there and it can be hard to absorb it all. The important thing is that you know the highlights, and use the resources that we have in today's world to make the information easier for you to access.

Alex is taking the time to learn about his vehicle online. There are endless resources to gain both visual and practical knowledge about your car. Depending on what type of learner you are, you might want to see a video of someone describing each part of the car, not read about it. Alex is using his strength of online research to get the information he needs and summarize it or himself.

Whether the vehicle you are using is yours, or your parents, you need to be familiar with the symbols, warning lights and sounds that may come up. Start with downloading the PDF manual for your vehicle onto your phone to have as a backup in case the paper version is missing out of your vehicle or it goes missing.

Skim through and see your familiarity with the symbols in the manual. If there is anything that you don't recognize, make sure to read about them. The majority of newer vehicles are very user friendly and reading the symbols is not difficult. It's just a matter of taking the time to know what they mean so that you aren't trying to frantically figure it out in an emergency.

Another great thing to do is to search online about your vehicle to see what other driver's say. Most vehicles have similar issues within their own make and model, so by knowing what typical issues arise, it can better prepare you for instances that happen.

I searched "common issues with a dodge journey", to see what would come up. On the website repairpal.com owners of Dodge Journeys reported problems and gave comments about what happened. The most common problem is that the keyless remote entry sometimes did not work. There were also reports about an over-heating engine due to debris in the cylinder head coolant port and dampness inside the vehicle caused by water leaks. ("Dodge Journey Problems and Complaints - 12 Issues")

This quick search gave me a lot of valuable information if I were going to be driving a dodge journey. You can also look up YouTube videos to access videos that will show you what sounds may be indications of trouble within your vehicle. You can most likely even find a quick 10-15 min video of a summary by someone very knowledgeable about your specific vehicle and its manual that will help you learn everything you need to know about your car.

The resources that you have access to in today's world are unbelievable. Take advantage of all of them and you will be a better and more informed driver overall.

Parent Tip: We don't love to admit this as parents, but when it comes to technology you are so much smarter than we are. You probably have the ability to learn more about the vehicle I drive in about 10% of the time.

One of my nephews made himself a quick reference guide for his truck using online resources and an app on his phone. It took him about 30 min and his parents were so surprised. It was informative, helpful, and showed them just how resourceful he could be. If you are using your parents' vehicle, try creating something like this and send them a copy. They will probably use it for themselves.

On your quick guide sheet you will want to include:

- pictures of lights that may appear on your dash and what they mean
- common issues associated with your vehicle
- a maintenance schedule. Put reminders on approximate dates in your phone to make sure you stay on top of it. We will talk more about your maintenance schedule shortly.
- Phone numbers for roadside assistance, tow trucks, and your mechanic or dealership
- Instructions for basic maintenance you can perform yourself such as a tire change, fluid top ups, and filter replacements.

WHAT DOES REGULAR MAINTENANCE LOOK LIKE?

I keep referring to keeping your vehicle maintained on a regular basis. You might have no idea what I am talking about. Let's jump back a bit and go over what a regular maintenance schedule looks like. Your owner's manual will give you one for your vehicle, but I want to familiarize you with the general idea and the terms.

Oil Changes

Your vehicle needs regular oil changes. This is the maintenance that you will get done the most in the life-time of your vehicle. Depending on the age, make and model of your vehicle it usually ranges between 5000-7500 miles or 6 months. Whichever comes first depending on how much you drive.

Your options for getting your oil changed are learning how to do it yourself, that can be very economical. Going through a quick lube service. Or taking it to a dealership or mechanic.

Filter Changes

Earlier we went over the different types of filters and the regularity that they need to be changed

Tire Maintenance

Don't forget to stay on top of your tires to check both their pressure and their tread. Over time your tire tread will wear down. Your tread is what keeps your grip to the road and prevents you from sliding all over the place. Especially in various types of precipitation. When your tread gets low, it will be time to change your tires. Depending on your driving habits and the quality of your tires, it can range anywhere from 40,000 – 80,000 miles. To prolong the life of your tires, you can rotate them 1-2 times each year. I think I had been driving at least 2 years before I knew what a tire rotation was. I honestly thought it had to do with how the tire was attached to the vehicle. What it actually means is moving the front tires to the back and the back tires to the front. The way your vehicle moves, it wears the tires differently on the front and the back. By rotating them, they are wearing in different spots and will hence last longer.

Lights

Check your turn signals, headlights, interior lights, hazard lights and brake lights regularly to make sure none of them are burnt out. Most newer vehicles will alert you if a light is not working properly, but it is always important to check with your own eyes as well.

Transmission Fluid

Your transmission fluid is similar to engine oil in that it helps lubricate your engine to keep things moving properly. Depending on your vehicle, you will eventually have to change out the transmission fluid. This is not done at the same frequency as your oil changes.

Transfer Case Fluid

In four wheel and all wheel drive vehicles, you will have a transfer case. Your vehicle manual will tell you how often you need to have this replaced, but it won't be very often.

Shocks and Struts

Your shocks and struts are part of your alignment system that allow you to be comfortable in your vehicle and not bouncing all over the place. They absorb the bumps and roughness of the road so you can steer your vehicle with ease. They don't need to be replaced that often, but should be inspected approximately every 50,000 miles. They can be damaged with rough roads or accidents, but with just regular wear and tear they should last you a long time.

Coolant Flush and Exchange

Your coolant is the fluid that keeps your engine calm, cool and collected. It prevents it from overheating. Regular checks and top ups to your coolant fluid levels should be performed. Overtime, there may be build up of debris and contaminants and the old coolant won't be able to do its job properly. Having it flushed out and replaced with fresh coolant will prevent wear on your engine.

Alignments

Your vehicle will get out of alignment sometimes if you have been driving on bumpy roads, or with just regular use. If your car is in alignment it will drive in a straight line without your hands on the steering wheel. When the alignment is out, it will veer to one side. Once a month, go to an empty parking lot and drive slowly in a straight line. Let go of the steering wheel with your hands hovering just above where you can grab it. See if you keep going in a straight line or start to drift to one side. A car that is out of alignment can be dangerous or steering as well as will wear your tires unevenly.

Brake Pads

Your brake pads help cushion the act of slowing down your vehicle. That's a lot of rubbing and pressure to put on any kind of material. Over time they will wear down and need to be replaced. Having them inspected approximately once a year will keep you safe and driving responsibly.

Windshield and Windshield wipers

You might not think about this one, but the wipers do need to be replaced. It's pretty easy to tell when they need to be replaced. When they just aren't doing a very good job, it's time to get new ones. They can be purchased from local auto part shops and easily swapped out.

If you get chips in your windshield from rocks, make sure to get them filled right away. This will prevent them from spreading into a full crack. Once your windshield cracks and starts spreading, it can inhibit your ability to see clearly while driving and you will have to replace the whole windshield.

TYPES OF GASOLINE

Over your lifetime, you are going to drive many different kinds of vehicles. You might rent vehicles on vacation, drive a work vehicle, own your own, borrow your parents, etc. You might not need to know the full maintenance for every vehicle depending on how long you are driving it, but you will need to know what kind of gas it takes.

When you pull up to the gas station, there is usually a variety of types of gas. Putting the wrong one in your tank can lead to pretty expensive repairs. Different gas stations offer slightly varied products, but in general there is:

- **Diesel** - This pump is usually very clearly marked and has a slightly different nozzle. Chances are you won't question whether you need diesel or not, if you have a diesel vehicle you will know it. Other than large trucks, most passenger vehicles are not Diesel.
- **Unleaded** - Unleaded usually comes in "regular" or 87 octane, and "premium" or 91 or 93 octane.

The difference between the regular and premium unleaded gas is how it burns within your engine. Vehicles with larger and more powerful engines typically need a more premium fuel to keep the pressure and size of the engine running smoothly. Many vehicles run totally fine on the more economical "regular" fuel, but it's up to you to find out. Many vehicles have the information printed on the inside of the door or the owner's manual. It's always good to ask your parents if you are borrowing theirs, or the seller if you are buying your own vehicle.

THINGS TO KEEP AT HOME

Keep on top of your fluids and check them monthly to make sure there hasn't been any leaks that you were aware of. Fluids that you will want to purchase and keep at home for tops ups are:

- **ATF** – Automatic transmission fluid
- **Gas Line Antifreeze** – This is poured into your gas line to prevent gas from freezing during winter months. In some colder climates, antifreeze is already added to the gas at the station
- **Engine Coolant** – also called antifreeze. Not to be confused with gas line anti-freeze, they are two different products and should not be interchanged.

- **Power Steering Fluid**
- **Windshield washer fluid**

TROUBLESHOOTING NOISES IN YOUR CAR

Let's go over some of the noises that your car might make, and what they might mean. As I mentioned before, doing a quick online search will help alert you to common problems your vehicle might have. This will also work for hearing the noises. You can search for examples of what certain noises sound like so you can familiarize yourself with them in case they happen.

Online research is very helpful, but it is no replacement for experience. You will get to know your own personal car better than anyone else, and you will be able to tell when something feels or sounds off.

Your car will be like a good friend, you will be able to tell when it's unhappy, scared, angry or down. Every time you drive, make sure that you turn the radio down and listen for clicks, rattles, changes in engine tone, or irregularities as you accelerate and brake.

Noises When Braking

- Your pads may need replacing
- On of your brake components is worn out and needs replacing

Noises When coasting (neither accelerating or braking)

- Your wheel hub and/or bearings could be worn
- Damaged drive shaft
- Your tires have damage such as uneven wear or wrong pressure
- You are dragging something. Maybe you ran over a tree branch and are unknowingly dragging it along

For the reader living in snow climates, it can be build up of snow in your tires. That was an embarrassing one for me to learn. The first winter I had my license I was driving and heard this wobbling sound like I had a flat tire. I pulled over in a safe spot and called roadside assistance. I was being safe by not wanting to drive too far with damaged tires. I made the right call, but when the tow truck driver arrived and quickly kicked the snow off the inside of my tires and out of the wheel-well I felt a little silly. I got back on the road and the sound was completely gone.

Noises when accelerating

- Something with the external components of your engine are going bad. This can include the alternator, power steering, belt pulley, pretensioners, or serpentine belt. You do not need to have an in depth knowledge of what each of these car parts does, but now you know where they are in the vehicle in case a mechanic tells you that it needs replacing.

- Something with the internal components of your engine are needing replacement. This can include your valves, timing chain, pistons or rocker arms. These will need to be replaced to prevent engine failure

The first time something goes wrong with your vehicle it can be hard to come up with a word to describe the sound. Some really common descriptive terms that you will hear around a mechanic shop are:

- **Chirping or growling** – this will often refer to a metal on metal sound. For example if one of your wheel is loose or damage and the parts are rubbing up against each other as it spins around
- **Hissing** – Often a sound associated with an overheating engine.
- **Tapping or popping** – this will be sounds that you might hear coming from engine components that are malfunctioning
- **Rattling, flapping, or whining**. You might hear this coming from below the car because it is

echoing from somewhere else. Using these words to describe a sound can help a mechanic look for it and find the source.

- **Roaring** – When your engine sounds like it's working harder than it normally does as you accelerate it will be louder than usually and make a roaring sound.
- **Intermittently** – this is a great term that mechanics use a lot. Its when an issue you are having with your vehicle happens on and off. So if you hear a sound for a day or two and then it goes away for a couple days, and then comes back. This gives them the information that they might need to take it for a couple different drives to determine the issue.

SOME OTHER GOOD HABITS AND TIPS:

After all this information you definitely will understand why we started this chapter by pointing out that you need to take good care of your vehicle so that it can take good care of you. Vehicles need a lot of upkeep to make sure they operate correctly and it's up to you to make sure they get that care.

Some additional good habits that you will want to form to prolong the life of your vehicle are:

1. Try not to let your fuel get too low. At the bottom of your fuel take, dirt and sediment will build up overtime. If you let your fuel get low before every single fill up, you will end up injecting all of that buildup into your fuel lines which can cause clogs in the injectors and it is bad for your fuel lines.
2. Remove excess items from your vehicle. Don't haul around heavy items for days at a time because you keep forgetting to take them out. It will lower your fuel consumption and can cause damage to your interior.
3. After a mechanic changes your parts, make sure to always ask for the old parts to keep. Not all parts are bad and in an emergency you could re-use them or even possibly resell them on eBay.

Now that you see the amount of maintenance that goes into a vehicle you can understand why I recommend you make yourself a schedule and stay on top of it. In addition to giving you regular reminders, a schedule can also help you create a budget. When you are making your maintenance schedule, call around to a few places or do some research online to see how much each of these items costs for your vehicle. It can be a little overwhelming at first, but between maintenance, insurance, and gas, not to mention the price of the vehicle itself, being a driver is not cheap and you need to be aware of it.

One last thing to remember about maintenance is how often you will need to get maintenance done is how much you drive. If you only drive your car on the weekend because you use public transit to get to school, then your maintenance isn't going to be as much. However, if you are doing a long commute every day plus driving yourself to extracurriculars, then your maintenance will need to be done more frequently.

Parent Tip: If you are going to be sharing your parents vehicle, offer to chip in for expenses every once in a while. If you are young, living at home and don't have a job yet, offer to help in other ways. An example would be, you might not have the money to pay for the oil change, but offer to take the vehicle for one to save your parents some time. Also making a maintenance schedule for your parents and shopping around online to find the best prices would be very appreciated by your parents.

4

YOUR LIFE AS A NEW DRIVER

"When driving, don't be right, be smart!"

— ANONYMOUS

I remember when my daughters first got their license, the groans and moans about putting up the new driver's license symbol. They didn't want to hang the sign in the vehicle, saying that it was embarrassing and that people would laugh at them.

Alex has a different perspective of the new driver's side. He thinks you should look at it as a superpower and take advantage of the time that you can use it. Other drivers are going to treat you differently, be very patient with you, and go out of their way to make it easier for you on the road. Not many drivers can say that they have that ability. You have to remember, most driving is about expectations of what the other cars will do, it's to your advantage to warn others that you may need some more time to react.

Experienced drivers know that new drivers don't have the same level of experience and ability to react to different situations. In general, drivers are going to give new drivers a little bit more leeway and understanding. They go out of their way to make it easier on the road for them. Especially because no one wants to be responsible for creating an accident with a new driver. It doesn't take much to get a new driver stressed and the chances of getting into an accident with a new driver if you're driving rashly or irresponsibly around them is higher than with an experienced driver. So hang that new driver's Sign proudly, and take advantage of the time you get with it.

BEING A NEW DRIVER IS EASY......RIGHT?

With your new drivers sign hanging in your back window, you are about to embark out on the road with all of your new skills learned from driving school and time behind the wheel with other trusted driver's. You got this!

For the most part you will have this. No doubt about it, but let's talk about what being a new driver looks like when things go wrong. Driving solo for the first little while can be stressful. Your first time alone in a busy city, you may think you're prepared but it takes time to get really used to all of the stimulus and different situations you'll encounter. Things don't always go according to the textbook, and you want to set yourself up to be comfortable when things can possibly go a little differently than you anticipated.

Alex just drove this route last week with a more experienced driver. Now that he is in the car alone, he feels like there are more street signs, more people, the buildings are bigger, and the cars are much faster. He's overwhelmed and that's without anything going wrong.

In the beginning, even after you get your license, if you were still slightly uncomfortable, there's no rush to drive alone or in a busy downtown situation. Spend time driving with more experienced drivers and in less busy areas to practice your skills and build upwards to being more comfortable driving alone.

Some times of day or situations are more dangerous to drive in than others. Some examples of higher stress or dangerous times are rush-hour, especially in the evening, Saturdays, large events or highways on summer holidays and long weekends. Think about different times and situations of driving as a video game. Sometimes it is an easy difficult level, and other times it is an advanced difficulty level. Determine your ability as a game player and choose a level that is appropriate for you. Only increase the times that you drive as a difficulty level when you feel like your skills are there. Just like a video game.

WHAT TO DO WHEN THINGS GO SIDEWAYS

What do I mean when I say things go sideways? Let's look at an example. When you're driving slowly in the city and doing a lot of stopping and starting, you might not realize that this puts a lot of stress on your engine. Your engine giving out in the middle of traffic is something that can happen and it's probably happened to most drivers at least once.

If your engine gives out in the middle of a busy street in the middle of a crowded downtown, it can be very stressful and you may easily get flustered or panic so let's talk about what you can do to handle this type of situation.

When your engine stops "under your watch" for the first time, take a deep breath and just let the other drivers honk. As a side note this again is where a new driver side would come in handy because people might be more patient knowing that this is probably the first time your engine has broken down and that you're most likely young and need some help. You might have other drivers quickly jumping out to help you knowing that you might not be totally comfortable with what's going on.

First patiently try to restart your engine as you always do. It may just start and you can apologetically wave out your window to the other driver's and move one. They might still honk and be frustrated with you, but good manners never hurt.

If your engine starts but keeps cutting out after a few feet, try to pull to the side to unblock traffic. You should never violate traffic rules but If you are in trouble, it's ok to pull over to the side. Make sure to put your hazards on so drivers know your vehicle is stopped and not working properly. Otherwise they may just think you are parking there and get really mad.

When your vehicle is unable to start, and you're stuck right in the middle of the street, There's no way around it, that just sort of stinks. You just have to try and make the best of the situation, do it safely, and try and remember that a lot of other drivers have been stuck in the situation as well. It will be over before you know it.

First thing you have to do is switch on your emergency/hazard lights. This as mentioned above will alert the drivers passing you, that something is wrong. Don't keep attempting to start the vehicle, because you don't want to drain the battery. If it doesn't start after a couple of tries, the vehicle needs a mechanic to assess it.

If you happen to have a passenger with you, ask them to get outside the car and guide the traffic behind you to move around your vehicle. If you don't have a passenger with you, and it's safe to do so, you can also get out and conduct the traffic after you call for the nearest traffic police you can reach. If possible, ask them to block the road for you. In case you were unable to move your vehicle and have to wait for a tow truck.

Alex is seen here directing traffic around his vehicle with a flat tire. If you want to be extra prepared, you can always keep a couple of small traffic cones and a reflective vest in case you have car trouble in the evening. Alex was thinking ahead and was very grateful to have these items so he could direct traffic and then change his tire once help arrived.

Ask people around you or if a vehicle asks if you need any help to push the car to the nearest shoulder of the road where you aren't blocking traffic. If you don't have a passenger with you, ask someone else to direct traffic while you and other people push the vehicle to safety.

Alex is seen here asking for help and as a group together safely moving his vehicle that broke down. Remember how I said when I first got my license that I felt like I had joined a cool club? Being a driver is kind of like that. We all want to share the road together safely and help each other out when we need it. Alex asked for help and was very grateful and polite to the people that helped him. Plus he knows he would do the same for them.

For the people that have helped you, always make sure to show them appreciation, because they didn't have to stop to help you, but they did.

If you're on the highway and you're moving don't hit the break immediately let the vehicle slow itself by gradually hitting the break. When you have slowed to a safe pace, try to pull the car onto the side with your hazard lights on. Check and see if it's safe to leave your car. In the worst case that you collide with another car, after you stop, wait with your seatbelt on until everything is quiet for 60 seconds longer. Then see if you know what's wrong or call for help. Keep the car visible to other drivers at all times.

Every driver knows that unforeseen situations happen. They aren't the most fun to deal with and it really can wreck your day, but they do happen to everyone. You just have to remain calm and handle the situation as quickly as possible. Also remember to not take it personally if other drivers get angry. Chances are they're in a rush to be somewhere and they're just a bit annoyed, and they don't stop to think about how yelling or honking can affect you. They forget that you are also having a not so great day and definitely didn't plan this.

I remember one time I was leaving a baseball game, and I didn't notice that my vehicle had a flat tire. This was an example of how I didn't do a walk around on my vehicle, and lived to regret it. I pulled out of my parking spot, and drove about 3 meters into a busy traffic lane of other vehicles also trying to leave the baseball game. I noticed the sound that my tire was making and realized that the front end of my vehicle was sloping forward. I threw my hazards on and got out of the vehicle to check. My tire was completely flat and I was unable to move my vehicle. So there I was blocking an entire lane of traffic of thousands of people trying to get out of a baseball game with a flat tire. My heart sank. I had a lot of angry people screaming, honking and yelling at me while I tried to change my tire as quickly as I could. The thing to remember, in that situation I wanted to make sure I still did the job properly to ensure that my vehicle was safe to drive out of the parking lot. It took a lot of patience for me to not get flustered and upset in such a bad situation. But I got through it, and I'm sure I'll never see any of those people again that I was so embarrassed in front of.

No matter how safe and Careful you are as a driver, and no matter how great of maintenance you do on your vehicle, situations will arise as a driver that you have to be calm and deal with, in the moment. Experience will allow you to handle them differently as you get older, but for now reading and learning as best you can from other drivers, will make the situation easier.

In some states or countries, you can take something called an advanced driver's course. In this environment you'll get to do exercises and find the edge of car control but the carefully managed environment that minimizes any risk to you or others. Decision-making behind the wheel, skid control, all those things are a part of this kind of course. As you get experience in that kind of environment and also get the confidence to sit behind the wheel when you're driving on the street.

These courses are often instructed by police class one drivers and writers so you're dealing with the very best professional drivers possible. In some situations to keep even reduce your insurance. Premiums because you'll get a rebate as a lower risk driver.

When I was young and learning how to drive, the driving instructor used to do one tactic that was similar to this type of driving. The area where I grew up had a lot of rural and highway roads around it, and knowing that new drivers will be spending a lot of time in this environment, the driving instructors would instruct us to slow the pace of the vehicle on the highway, and without warning would grab the wheel and run us into the ditch. It was valuable because you were able to see what your reaction would be in that situation. This was a less than safe tactic that has now been updated and advanced driving lessons take the place in a more controlled environment. The old-school way that I had to deal with was rather unsafe, and now you have resources that can make it just as effective but in a better environment.

ARE YOU A SHY DRIVER?

Something to consider, if you are still struggling about a fear of driving is if driving is right for you. Are you still finding yourself having resistance to get behind the wheel after you get your license? Driving is not necessary for every lifestyle, so check your motivations. Resolve to drive only when the best available motive is transportation. Walking, cycling and public transit, or just not making the trip may be better alternatives.

If you would like to drive, take a moment to consider all the positive feelings that driving can give you. Don't let any worries or thoughts drive your way from achieving your goal or being a good driver who enjoys the ride. Being a shy driver does it mean that you should quit trying to learn. Taking extra lessons and driving with experienced drivers will eventually get you to a level you want to be. I have 100% confidence in you. I just want you to know that if you just feel like driving is not going to become a comfortable and safe way for you to get around then you don't need to feel pressure to do it at any time.

5

WHEN DRIVE, YOU CAN'T CONTROL THE WEATHER

"Adventure is worthwhile in itself"

— AMELIA EARHART

W hen you're first starting out, if you're not familiar with certain weather conditions such as ice, rain, snow, hail, or fog, try to avoid driving alone in this type of weather. If you see that there's light snow out this is a great chance for you to go and practice with a more experienced driver.

However, there will be times when you're already on the road or you need to get home, and certain weather arises that you weren't prepared for or haven't driven in, and you need to have the mindset that you can handle this. Much like driving at certain times of the day like rush-hour or at night, driving in certain weather conditions can be extremely harrowing to a new driver and can lead to dangerous situations.

The biggest thing to remember is that your car is built to keep you safe in all types of weather conditions. It's your job as a driver to also drive safely to keep yourself and others on the road safe. Speeding for example when it's icy out is a terrible idea, and quite easily leads to accidents.

The rule of thumb is to adapt your driving in two ways:

1. Slow Down
2. Increase the distance between you and the car in front of you

In all situations Alex keeps a safe distance between him and the vehicle in front of him. He knows that if the weather starts to turn bad, he would double the distance between him and other cars because of delayed reaction times of him and his vehicle.

TYPES OF WEATHER

Snow

We all love different types of weather for a variety of reasons. Alex loves the winter because who doesn't love getting cozy next to the fire? On this particular evening, Alex didn't realize that a snow storm had started while he was enjoying time with friends. He didn't have a choice but to drive home, and, thankfully, he had been practicing winter driving to be prepared for just this type of situation.

Many people may never have to drive in snow in their entire lives. For example if you grow up in Florida and stay in the southern states, you may never encounter driving in snow. It really does take its own set of skills. Every year when it snows, I swear it takes at least 2 to 3 weeks for people to remember that you can't drive the same on dry roads as you do with snow roads.

Snow can make things very tricky because the roads will be slippery or, if it's heavy sticky snow, your wheels turn and react differently than on dry roads. As well, even things like parking you have to take into consideration because you can get stuck in the snow and unable to safely pull your vehicle out on the road. Everyone who grows up in heavy snowfall cities has had the joy of digging a car out and/or needing help to push it out of a snowbank.

Driving very slow in heavy snow is important to get to your destination safely. Also, being extra aware of other driver speeds and how they are driving will help you stay safe. A great example would be your start time when you're approaching a stop sign is much longer in the snow than it is on dry roads. Heavily driven roads often turn icy because the heat of the vehicle tires melt the snow enough that it's wet, and then the cold weather freezes it. Driving on ice can often lead to skidding. Your reactions automatically slow down not because of your reaction time but how your vehicle can respond in this condition.

This is a good time to remind you about the extra things you should carry with you in the car during the snowy and winter months. Alex has his full winter gear with him, as well you should carry a candle, sand or kitty litter, a first aid kit, and a warm blanket.

Rain

Rain can pop up out of nowhere, and when it's very heavy, can make driving really difficult due to decreased visibility. Alex is driving home from school, and it starts to lightly drizzle. He is finding it difficult because the sun is also shining and reflecting off the water. He knows to follow the rule of slowing down and increasing the distance between him and other drivers. If his visibility gets worse, he makes a plan to pull over and safely wait the rain out in a parking lot.

As we discussed earlier, rain can be difficult to drive in, because there is a danger of hydroplaning. Keeping your tire pressure at an appropriate level will keep you safe when it starts to rain heavily. Also making sure that you have good windshield wipers that don't need replacing, will help your visibility, and prevent you from getting into an accident.

If the rain starts and it's so heavy that you're unable to see vehicles in front of you, find a safe place to pull over and park. This doesn't mean the shoulder of the road, because if you can't see other vehicles, they can't see you. If you're on the highway try to find a designated turn out. If you're in the city try to find a parking lot, or a side street that doesn't have heavy traffic. Try to wait out the rain until you are comfortable with your visibility and can safely operate your vehicle to get home.

Even with the best intentions, our vehicle doesn't always perform the way we hope it will. Alex is driving in the rain, and although his car is well maintained, and he is driving slowly, his vehicle starts to hydroplane. If this happens to you, let off the gas pedal slowly and steer straight until you gain control. If your car starts to spin, turn your wheel in the direction that the vehicle is spinning, slowly. You will most likely get an adrenaline rush. Don't let this panic you or make uncontrolled motions. Do not turn your wheel against the direction it has begun to spin, or sharply jerk the wheel from one side to the other. Alex smoothly and calmly turns the wheels in the direction of his spin and regains control of the vehicle so he can safely pull it to the side of the road and turn his hazard lights on to take a minute to regain his composure too. He kept himself safe and looked like a professional drifter in the process.

Freezing rain

This may be one of the most dangerous types of weather to drive-in.

Many people assume that extremely cold weather would be the toughest, but in very cold weather the roads end up being quite dry. Any ice on the road has been driven over enough that it dissipates and disappears from the roads, and the cold air is actually quite dry.

It's when the temperature hovers around freezing so that there's precipitation, but it's cold enough to quickly freeze it, that there's large amounts of slippery ice or sometimes what's called black ice that is out on the roads. Black ice is when it's very clear so you can't distinguish the difference between the black road and the ice itself, so you can't see it coming. It's quite common on highways. Being aware of icy roads and how to drive on them is extremely important. Highway driving in freezing rain can be extra dangerous because there isn't the infrastructure set up to put salt and or gravel on the roads the way they do in the city to make the roads more grippy in icy conditions.

If you find yourself in a situation where you are sliding on ice, performing the same motions as when you are hydroplaning. Let your foot off the gas pedal and steer straight to gain control of the vehicle. Resist the temptation to hit the brakes with a hard stop. Tap the brakes very lightly and turn into the direction of the spin if your vehicle starts to turn. Stay calm and keep your movements smooth and controlled.

Fog

Driving in fog is also extremely challenging and can be very difficult for a new driver. Fog can block your visibility, so that you are unable to react to other vehicles and or stay on the path of the road safely. You may miss things like street signs, stop signs, coming up to street lights quicker than you anticipated, or if a pedestrian steps out on the road and you don't see them in advance to react accordingly. Same goes for wildlife running out onto the road. Avoid driving in heavy fog as much as possible as there is no way to safely navigate when your visibility is extremely low.

For light fog, your vehicle is equipped with fog lights that point your headlights at a different angle to try and help you see farther than pointing them head-on. However in heavier denser fog there's only so much that the fog lights can accomplish. And you still won't be able to see very well.

Take advantage of different weather conditions that come up if you have the time to go out with a more experienced driver and practice. For example if a light snowfall happens, and you're just sitting around your parents, ask them if you can go for a 10 to 20 minute drive to practice driving in the snow. It's great because they can give you tips like how to start raking farther away from stop signs and looking for different types of ice.

Different Lighting

Sunlight at sunrise and sundown. A romantic moment at the beginning and the end of the day. If you find yourself behind the steering wheel at these times, take good care. Your vision can have trouble adjusting to new lighting, and you may see things slightly differently and not quite as clearly. Make sure to keep sunglasses in your car to help your vision during bright lighting.

At these times of day you might be prone to encounter drowsy drivers. Or worse, you might be one of them. Resting is the only solution to this problem. Coffee and energy drinks might make you feel more energetic, but your body will still need rest, and your reaction time will be slower than normal. I remember one time when I was young, I was visiting a friend in another city, and I left after a fairly sleepless night to drive home. I very quickly realized that I was too tired to drive three hours home. I happened to be right by the airport, so I pulled into the parking lot and took a long nap in my car until I felt rested enough to drive safely.

At nighttime, some people have more trouble driving in the dark than others. I remember my mom always saying she had "terrible night vision" and didn't like driving after dark. I always thought that was strange because I had no trouble seeing at night. Now that I'm getting older, I'm finding myself struggling a bit more, and I understand what my mom was saying. I now plan longer drives and trips around daytime driving because I'm not as confident as I used to be at nighttime.

Finally, different lighting can make it difficult to see things on the road such as wildlife. Wildlife, such as deer, is another cause for concern during the twilight hours. Especially on open roads and rural highways, animals prefer to come out during dusk and dawn, and it's not unusual to see them run across the road at this time. A valuable thing that my dad taught me is that if you see one animal, chances are there are more. So even though I see one deer run safely across the road as I was approaching, it doesn't mean he won't have a friend approaching the road right after you are driving by. So the second you see any wildlife near the road, check your rearview mirror to see if there is a vehicle behind you and start to slow your pace for a few miles so that you can stop quickly if needed. Just keep an eye on any traffic behind you and turn your hazards on if you are slowing down a lot.

STAYING CALM

Alex is taking a deep breath and collecting himself to stay calm. This tactic can be used in a variety of situations to calm your nerves so use it when you need it.

The biggest factor in all weather and various imperfect driving situations is to stay calm and use good judgement. Even if you are desperate to get somewhere, if the weather is too unsafe, don't drive. If you feel uncomfortable while driving, don't put yourself or other driver's at risk by pushing through.

Parent Tip: If bad weather strikes and you have a curfew, your parents will prefer you be safe rather than home on time. Give them a call and let them know you aren't comfortable driving, and together come up with an alternate plan to get you home safely. Perhaps you might have to stay the night at a friend's house or wait for them to come pick you up. They will be much happier that you made the judgement call about your abilities than struggling to get home unsafely.

6

THE THREE DS THAT LEAD TO DEATH ON WHEELS

"It's better to lose a minute in your life, than your life in a minute"

— URUGUAYAN PROVERB

Alex is following his philosophy of "groom before you zoom." He developed this tactic when he realized he was spending time in his vehicle looking in the mirror, trying to get himself ready for school while driving. He was trying to multitask, but after a near fender bender, he realized that what he was doing was very unsafe. He was participating in distracted driving, which is one of the three deadly Ds of driving. Now he makes sure he has nothing to take his attention off the road.

When you get behind the wheel of your vehicle, it is your responsibility as a driver to make sure you are in coherent physical condition and focused on the road and the vehicles around you. If you choose to behave differently, you are not only putting yourself at risk, but everyone in your vehicle and the vehicles around you. This also includes pedestrians near the road too.

It's very easy for me to say "Don't drink and drive", or "Pay attention on the road," but I want to get deeper into the reason why.

THE THREE DS: DRUNK, DRUGGED, AND DISTRACTED

Drinking and Driving

Everybody knows that drinking and driving is one of the worst things you can possibly do. When you see commercials or hear the phrase "don't drink and drive" can I ask if it resonates with you? At this point it might not. You don't drive yet, and you are too young to have any experience with alcohol to understand how it impairs your ability to think clearly, react quickly to situations, or even behave in a responsible manner. It's hard for you to understand how serious it is.

So without experience with either drinking or driving, you might now understand how putting the two together is a combination for horrific consequences.

I'm going to try and give you an analogy so you can understand why it's not an option and never should be.

Let's say you were standing on a sidewalk on a bright sunny clear day in the middle of the afternoon. I put $100 on a table 20 feet in front of you and tell you that you have 10 min to get to it and if you do, you could keep it. You would be very confident that you could walk 20 feet with no distractions and pick up the $100 in 20 sec, not to mention the remaining time you would have to do it. This is the equivalent to a sober driver with confident skills driving in a safe manner.

Now let's say you are standing on that same sidewalk in the evening at dusk. It's foggy and your glasses are very dirty. You are having trouble seeing even 2 feet in front of you. I give you a map with poor directions and tell you that you have 2 min to find $10,000 on a table 100 feet away and you have to follow the poor map. You would be frantic and running all over the place running into things and probably wouldn't make the 2 min deadline. Plus you might really hurt yourself in the process if you ran onto the road or fell while sprinting in the fog and looking at your map. This is the equivalent to an intoxicated driver and how they can react and maneuver in the car when they should not be operating it.

Now let's put this analogy into a real life situation that you may experience. In this scenario you are at a friend's house with a bunch of friends who are drinking. You know that you will be driving home in a few hours because your parents gave you a curfew of 10pm.

In the first possibility you leave your friend's house sober at 930 to give yourself lots of time to safely drive home. You aren't rushing and you have a clear head. This is similar to you being able to easily grab the $100 in clear conditions. It's easy money and you know you can do it safely and quickly. The same as driving home calmly, with clear focus, and having your wits about you.

Now in the second scenario let's pretend you tell your parents you will be home by 10pm, but this time you don't leave yourself enough time and know you are going to be late, plus you and your friends thought it would be cool to try having a beer or two. It might not seem like very much alcohol but it is absolutely enough to impair your ability to drive safely. Now, all of a sudden you are frantically speeding home to not get in trouble, and everything that keeps you a safe driver is gone. You are speeding because the alcohol removes your inhibitions and you don't want to get into trouble. You don't have your regular judgement, awareness or response time because of your impairment. All of these factors can equate to you putting your life and other people in danger. You could die or kill someone else. That is a statement that you really need to think about. I will repeat, driving under the influence of any alcohol or drugs can cause you to kill yourself or someone else. This situation is similar to you running around in the fog trying to find that $10,000. You are frantic because that is a lot of money, and you don't have much time, but you are putting your safety at risk trying to find it.

Parent Tip: Any parent would be happy with you if you called and told them the truth. They may punish you, but they will respect you and go easier on you if you call them and simply say " Mom and Dad, I did something stupid tonight, I experimented with drugs or alcohol and I don't feel safe to drive. Can you please come get me?" The small amount of lecturing you get is so worth the exchange of hurting someone or worse.

Alex knows that driving under the influence is an absolute no-no. He knows that this is what a driver might look like that thinks they are going straight. Driving under impairment makes you feel like you are driving properly, but in actuality you aren't.

Drugs and Driving

In many states, it's not even just drinking anymore, it's driving under the influence since legalized marijuana is illegal to ingest and operate a vehicle as well. As we talked about with drinking, you presumably don't have any experience with the effects of drugs and especially not how they will affect your driving ability.

What's even worse about drugs is that at this time there isn't a quick test such as a breathalyzer that authorities can use to detect usage if you are stopped. So often people think they can "get away" with driving under the influence of drugs, or that it is somehow safer. It is by no means safer and also impairs your judgement, clarity, and reaction time the way alcohol does.

The consequences to driving under the influence of either alcohol or other substances depends on state to state, but you do not want to be an offender. You can lose your license, face criminal charges, and, in the case where you cause an accident, you can be sentenced to jail time. When you think about how serious that is, having a drink or indulging in recreational drug use just doesn't seem worth it does it?

Always plan ahead and think about how you and your friends will safely get home. Plan for alternative transportation before you head out for an evening that you may not be able to safely drive home. Keep in mind that I am referring to those individuals that are legally able to participate in these activities. Another thing you can do as a responsible driver is offer to be the designated driver for the night. You offer to stay sober so you can make sure all your friends get home safely.

Distracted Driving

Make your phone calls before and after you drive. Alex is finishing up chatting with a friend before getting behind the wheel. Even when you use Bluetooth, talking on the phone distracts you and makes your driving unsafe.

Distracted driving is a term that refers to a lot of different things. Basically it's anything that will prevent you from fully concentrating on your driving. You want to have your hands busy with the steering wheel and your eyes staring at the road, everything else you can do either before or after you start driving.

Remember earlier in the book I mentioned the dangers of cell phone usage in the vehicle and how it should be your priority to store it somewhere out of reach, distracted driving is the reason. In 2020, there were 1.6 million accidents caused by texting and driving. It is estimated 25% of all accidents are caused by cell phone usage. Also in 2020, there were 4637 deaths related to texting and driving. (Nikola Djurkovic). Those are some pretty staggering statistics for something that is so unavoidable.

If there is something really pressing that you need to take care of on your phone, safely pull into a parking lot or designated turnout on the highway. Stop lights do not count as a safe time to respond to a text. Multi-tasking while driving is not smart. While you are at a stop light, you have to pay attention to vehicles around you. What if an emergency vehicle came up behind you and you were busy texting so you didn't move out of the way quickly. That's valuable seconds that someone is waiting for that vehicle to arrive, and you delayed them because you weren't paying attention.

Alex is busy multitasking at his desk. He is an excellent multitasker but knows he has to get everything done before he leaves to drive home. His mind needs to focus on getting home safely and not sending emails from his phone because he didn't get it done at work.

Another type of distracted driving is playing with the radio or different settings in the vehicle. If you are a focused driver, of course you can listen to music safely in the vehicle, but make sure you aren't taking your eyes off the road to change the station or looking for a specific song. Make a playlist before you leave so you can listen to all of your favorite tunes without making your driving unsafe.

Eating is also a distractor that takes your hands off the wheel. Not to mention if you spill something hot it could cause you to react and lose control of the vehicle. Even a slight swerve as you jump from spilling ketchup on your new white shirt could cause you to collide with another vehicle. Not really worth it when you could just pull over and eat before you leave.

What To do When Other Drivers Participate in the 3 Ds.

When it comes to the three Ds of unsafe driving, you have the ability to make smart decisions based on your own actions, but what do you do when other driver's make bad decisions?

I think everyone at some point in time in their driving career may be put in a situation where they feel uncomfortable. This can happen because someone you know is attempting to drive under the influence, or you spot someone on the road that is driving irregularly and looks like they could cause an accident. So what do you do in this scenario?

If someone you know is driving under the influence, it can be very tricky. It sounds easy enough to simply say to a friend that they should think about taking alternative transportation, but when you are put in that position it can be very difficult. You don't want to risk losing a friendship or create a scene and embarrass them. It's really tough. Here are a few things you can do to keep everyone safe and diffuse a situation:

1. Offer to drive them home if you are sober and have not been drinking. Tell them you will come back with them and get their car tomorrow. If they are really worried that their parents will be mad about their car not being there, and will get in trouble, offer to leave your car and drive them home in theirs. Call your parents and ask them to meet you there to pick you up. They will be so happy with your responsibility they won't be mad. You don't know your friend's situation and maybe they haven't had as open of communication as you and yours.

2. If you are paying for a ride home, offer for them to come with you. Even tell them they can crash at your house.

3. This one is a little extreme, but I did see it used successfully once when I was younger. I was at

a friend's house and there was a friend that had consumed a lot of alcohol. He was slurring his speech and not walking properly. He was busy looking for his keys and angrily yelling at people who were trying to prevent him from driving. While a few of us distracted him, someone went and let the air out of one of his tires. At that point even if he wanted to, he couldn't get his vehicle home.

If none of these tactics above work and you are unable to convince someone not to get behind the wheel who shouldn't be, you may need to try and take their keys away. This is really uncomfortable and stinks to be put in that situation. You have every right to be mad at someone for putting you in this position. If they absolutely refuse and take off, you may have to call authorities with a description of their vehicle and what direction they are heading. Telling on someone probably feels wrong and goes against every fiber in your being, but remember that you could be saving their life or someone else's.

It seems like every year around graduation time, tragic stories arise in the news about a car accident that takes the lives of a few students celebrating at their prom or other party. My sister lost a few of her closest friends who were hit by another car of students that were drinking and driving. Four kids lost their lives that night, and the driver who caused the accident lived. I didn't know him very well but I know that it changed his life forever and he will regret that decision forever.

You have the power to not put yourself in any vehicle that may result in this type of scenario, as a driver or passenger. You can also do your best to keep those around you safe as well. You can't control other drivers but you can do your best to be aware of their driving and avoid situations that could be potentially dangerous. We will move onto what I mean by this next.

MORE CAUSES OF UNSAFE DRIVING

Speeding

Quite often you will see commercials or signs on the road saying "speed kills." It absolutely does. It's something that is so unavoidable, but it's tempting, and the more confident driver's get over the years, they seem more and more comfortable with it. In 2019, it was recorded that 26% of traffic related deaths in the US were caused by speeding. That equated to 25 people a day. ("Speeding") How sad is that? 25 unnecessary deaths that could have been avoided if people just slowed down and reached their destination 5-10 minutes later.

Driving the speed limit might sound like an easy task, and easy to follow, but it can be hard when other driver's put pressure on you. Have you ever been driving on the highway when the speed limit is 55 mph and it seems like everyone is flying by you at 75 mph? You have driver's give you a dirty look as they drive by because you are going the speed limit and they are in a hurry to get around you and go faster. You may even have some other more experienced drivers tell you that you are going to cause an accident by going the speed limit when everyone else is going faster. This is false, and usually just said by people who like to speed. The driver's that are choosing to speed and go 75 mph are the one's creating a dangerous situation, and you don't need to feel pressure to participate in it.

You may even encounter a situation on a single lane road where a speeding driver comes up behind you and drive's really closely as to signal you to speed up. They may even honk to put pressure on you to get out of the way. DO NOT speed up. If you do speed up, you are increasing your chances of an accident. A better way to deal with it, is to create an opportunity for them to pass you. In the city, turn your signal light on and pull to the side to let them by. If you are on a one lane highway, turn your right signal light on and start to slow your vehicle as you pull towards the shoulder of the road. This indicates to them that you are pulling to the side to let them overtake you. This will diffuse the situation, and if they have any manners, they will give you a quick thank you wave as they pass on by.

Alex is displaying the speed limit sign to remind you how important it is to follow the speed limit rules. He knows the safety of driving the speed limit and the dangers of driving faster. To further display his point, Alex did a little math for you. Let's say you have a long road trip ahead of you that's 500 miles.

- If you drive 55 miles per hour it will take you 9 hours, 5 minutes, and 27 seconds
- If you drive 65 miles per hour it will take you 7 hours, 41 minutes, and 32 seconds.

This is obviously assuming that you kept that speed constant with no stops. Do you think the danger you are putting yourself in is worth the approximate hour-and-a-half you would save?

Now look at your daily commute. Let's pretend its 20 miles.

- If you drive 55 miles per hour, it will take you 21 minutes and 49 seconds
- If you drive 75 miles per hour, it will take you 16 minutes.

That's not even 5 minutes you would save to risk your life terribly every day! I promise you speeding is not worth it.

Emotional Driving

The way you feel can create changes in your driving habits. If you are happy and focused, you will find yourself in your safest driving mindset, but a lot of times we are dealing with other moods.

We will talk about road rage a bit more in chapter 8, but aggressive driving can be very dangerous if it's you or another driver on the road. We just talked about a driver getting frustrated with you for driving the speed limit, and driving too closely to you. If that person is extra angry, they may be honking and swearing and trying to intimidate you. This can be scary for a new driver. Or you might just get angry right back! Try not to let the other driver's emotions affect yours. You don't know what they are going through. Maybe it's a parent who just found out that their child was hurt at school and they are racing to get there and you are slowing them down. It doesn't make their speeding acceptable or any safer, but at least you can understand where emotion might be coming from. When another driver seems really angry, don't engage with them or be emotional back, just move to the side and let them by.

If you find yourself driving more aggressively because you are cranky or mad about something, maybe pull to the side of the road and give yourself a few minutes to cool down. Listen to a bit of music, or go into a coffee shop and have a drink. I know there have been situations where I was frustrated after a long day of work, and running late to something, which caused me to try and rush through traffic by weaving in and out of lanes trying to get ahead. It can be especially frustrating if a light turns green and you see someone sitting on their phone texting instead of paying attention, but you have to try and remind yourself that you won't get there much faster and you are putting yourself at risk for an accident.

Any emotion can cause you to drive differently. Maybe you just had a rough break up with a significant other and you are sad and teary which is causing you to be less aware of your surroundings, or with decreased visibility because you can't see clearly. Maybe you are anxious because you are nervous about a big presentation at school and you are jumpier and less calm while driving. Try your best to avoid driving in these situations, and arrange a different mode of transportation.

Parent Tip: This is another situation similar to driving under the influence that if you call your parent and let them know that you are really not comfortable driving due to an emotional state, they will not only come get you, but want to help you work through whatever you are upset about. Not to mention, it shows a lot of emotional maturity to make that call.

Passengers

This could also fall under the umbrella of distracted driving, but I felt it needed its own category to confirm its importance.

As soon as you get your license, you are going to want to show off your new skills to your friends. It's exciting! I remember as soon as I got my license, I drove straight to my best friend's house and we went to the movies. It was a big deal!

However as exciting as it is to have all your friends in the car, it can be a huge distraction. You are going to talk with each other, play music, and just have more interaction than if you were alone. Just imagine you are in rush hour traffic, music blaring, friends all chatting with each other, and one of them reads a text and yells out a reaction, not thinking about how it might surprise you and cause you to take your eyes off the road. Things like that happen, so it's just something to be aware of when you have other people in the car.

7

ENCOUNTERS WITH AUTHORITIES

"The best car safety device is a rear view mirror with a cop it in"

— DUDLEY MOORE

There are a lot of misconceptions of what an encounter with a police officer might look like. In the movies, people flirt with officers to get out of tickets, laugh at them, run away from them or even pretend to be police officers in some instances. Although it makes for some pretty entertaining screen time, in real life it's a bit different. For example, if you don't stop for a police officer and try to out drive them, they will catch you and you will be charged.

Although a police pull-over is nobody's favorite activity, chances are it's only happening if you are doing something wrong or in danger. Try to remember that they are there to keep us safe, not for the sole purpose of wrecking your day. Let's go over the steps in detail about what the police stop will look like and what your role as a driver is.

STEPS TO A POLICE PULL OVER

1. So you are driving along and suddenly you see the bright red and blue lights spinning in your rear view mirror. No matter how many times it happens in your life (which hopefully isn't many), your stomach does a flip flop and your heart begins to beat a little faster. Your first step is to calmly pull over to a safe spot. If you know of a nearby parking lot or a side street coming up, you are legally allowed to drive a little bit further before you stop the car.

a. If you are on an unsafe road to stop and pull over such as a two lane highway with a very narrow shoulder, start to slow and put your hazard lights on to let the police officer know you are looking for a safer spot such as a designated turn out to pull over. Remember they are the ones that have to get out of their vehicle so they want you to stop somewhere safe too.

b. When they approach your vehicle, explain to them that you saw them right away but wanted to stop somewhere a little safer for everyone.

2. After you are safely stopped, place your vehicle in park, roll down the window, and shut the car off. You can leave the power on, especially at nighttime for the lighting, but make sure to turn the engine off.

3. As the police officer approaches the vehicle, do not get out of the vehicle. Just wait until they approach your vehicle.

4. They will ask to see your license and registration of the vehicle. Earlier in the book I referenced always having these in your vehicle, and in a place where you can find them instantly. Don't be frantically searching around the vehicle and opening and closing things as they approach the vehicle. Wait until they ask for it, and then you can calmly open your glovebox and wallet/purse/bag, to get your license and registration. As they approach the vehicle, keep your hands at the top of your steering wheel and your seatbelt on. Remember that police officers approach all types of situations in vehicles, and even though you know that you aren't dangerous, they don't. By keeping your hands visible, and only looking for things when they ask you to, they can be confident that the situation is under control.

5. At this point in time, the police officer is going to tell you why they pulled you over. It could be because you were doing something wrong like speeding, you missed a stop sign, or have expired registration. You are human and you make mistakes, but you do have to pay the consequences. So don't get angry with the officer. Be polite, courteous, and respectful. Remember they are just doing their job.

6. Be truthful and communicate thoroughly as you talk with the officer. You might be uncomfortable, but the police officer knows it can be stressful for driver's, especially one that has the new driver sign hanging in their window. You don't have to be friendly, or engage in small talk if you don't want to, but being kind can go a long way and cooperating with their questions will get the whole process over with quickly.

7. Next the officer is going to take your license and registration and go back to their car to check out your information. They do this to see if you have any outstanding tickets, arrests, and any other relevant information. If it's winter, let them know you are going to restart your vehicle while they are gone for warmth. If you have anything else pressing make sure to make them aware of it. An example was one time when I was pulled over and had my two daughters in the car and they were quite young. I asked the officer if it was ok for me to get out of the vehicle to get some snacks out of the back to keep them entertained. They are obviously going to say yes, you just want to make them aware of your behavior. It might seem over the top but again remember that they don't know the difference between you and someone who may pull a weapon on them or take off. So don't give them any reason to think otherwise.

8. In the event that you are asked to get out of your vehicle, the process will look something like this:

  a. Exit the vehicle with both hands visible
  b. Only do what the officer asks you to do or say. For example, don't reach for your phone to text

someone that you are running late or try to take a picture for "a funny story" later. Chances are you will alarm or antagonize the officer which is not in your best interest.

c. It is probably embarrassing and a little scary if this happens, but remember that you are not in danger. Police cars have dash cams that are recording the entire interaction. This is an example of ways police are held accountable to their actions as well. They are also human and can make mistakes, and have varying personalities, but you staying calm and compliant is the easiest way to get through it.

9. This is a good time to discuss what your rights are as a driver. If the interaction is not sitting well with you, or something seems off, you have the right to:

a. Ask for the police officer's name and badge number.

b. If you feel that the officer is unprofessional, disrespectful, or violating one of your rights, you can demand a police supervisor to respond to the scene.

c. You have the right to record your interaction. Keep in mind this is for your safety and again not for entertainment, and do not under any circumstances post it online. Don't hold a phone in the officer's face, if the situation is already uncomfortable it will make it worse. Let them know you are recording because it is what you were taught to do by your driving instructor and parents.

d. Do not refuse an inspection of either your vehicle or physical pat down. And under no circumstances try to resist arrest. You have the right to remain silent, and discuss the events once you have a lawyer present who can help guide you through the situation and not make it worse.

e. If you disagree with the officer don't use your pull over time arguing and trying to change their mind. You will have your right to objections or defence later.

I'll give you an example of a time that I wish I had known my rights. I was driving home one evening after a late night class in university. I was driving straight through a green light, and midway through the intersection, the vehicle to the left of me turned right into the side of my vehicle. They had misread the street sign and thought they were in the lane that either go straight or turn. While we were waiting for the police to arrive, I heard them laughing as they told their friends on the phone that the girl driving had been drinking, and that they thought the whole thing was "epic". Insert eye roll here. When the police arrived, I asked them to please give us both a breathalyzer based on what I had heard. The police officer told me to "just let her to her job" and that it wouldn't be necessary. I also wasn't experienced enough to know that we shouldn't have moved our vehicles. We had both pulled to the side as to not block traffic, but then it was impossible to see who's fault it was. Unfortunately because there were no witnesses, we both were deemed at fault, and my insurance went up and I had to pay the deductible to have my vehicle fixed. Had I known my rights, I would have asked for a superior officer to come and do the breathalyzer and I never would have moved my car. It was an expensive lesson.

10. As you part ways after your pull over, assuming it's a simple routine stop, and you maybe have a fine for a minor traffic violation, make sure to thank the police officer and pull away only after they have told you that you are free to go. You might be thinking that I'm crazy to suggest that you thank them after they just gave you a ticket but again remember that they are just doing their job and you were the one not following the

rules. Try and think about it this way, let's say your job is a nurse. Everyday you go to work and deal with wonderful patients, who even though they are there because they have health issues that may be unlucky or self-inflicted, they make sure to show you appreciation because you are great at your job. This would motivate you to continue to be great at your job and go above and beyond for all these patients that are so kind to you and know you work hard. Now pretend all those same patients are awful to you. They think it's your fault they are sick, and your fault they had to wait in the waiting room so long, and that you enjoy their discomfort. They call you names, talk to you disrespectfully, and never bother to say thank you for your efforts. I'm guessing over time you would stop trying as hard, and grow to dislike your patients, and treat them all a little less nicely. Even when you had a nice person come in, you might be a bit jaded and not really care. Now try to think of what that police officer's day looks like. They are trying to help people and ensure they follow the law and people do nothing but curse at them or treat them like a nuisance. If more people apologized for breaking the law and thanked them for their time, maybe they would have a better job overall.

That being said, the world is not a perfect place, and

sometimes police officers can be a bit intimidating, so let's talk about the non-verbal piece of your interaction.

The Non-Verbal Aspect of a Police Pullover

Do you member how earlier in the book, I referenced how the way you take care of your vehicle says a lot about you? That sort of comes into play at this moment. Whether you like it or not, police officers are not perfect. They are well trained to not profile or have biases, but unfortunately it's part of human nature to make assumptions based on observations and past experiences. The best thing you can do to stay a safe driver, is give them no reason to make wrong assumptions about you.

Some of you are going to strongly disagree with me on this point, saying that it goes against your rights as a US citizen to be able to look, say and do whatever you want as long as it's legal. You are 100% correct. That is your right. However, I'll give you an example. If the police officer approaches your vehicle, and you have a large sticker in your back window that references the second amendment, which is your right to bear arms, the officer will most likely think that you're probably carrying a gun. This again is your right in certain states, but it will automatically put the police officer on edge.

They can't help that, they want to stay safe just as much as you do.

When I talked about how if the police officer sees the new driver sticker in your window, he will treat you differently in a positive way, when they see other indicators in your window, it's going to be a different approach that they may have with you.

I've seen bumper stickers, basically indicating someone peeing on a police officer, how much do you think that police officer really wants to pull that person over and interact with them, and what do you think the chances of that interaction going well are?

Even the physical condition of your car may play into how they observe you. If they see that your vehicle is well-maintained, the inside is neat and tidy, and you were quickly able to locate your license and registration because everything is so organized, they're going to assume that in general you are a fairly put together person that's going to follow the rules. They are going to make that assumption about you based on what they see.

That's not to say you need to have a vehicle in perfect condition, if what you can afford to drive is a bit of a rust bucket, that's OK, when they approach you and see that the inside of the vehicle is neat and organized they are going to make that same positive assumption.

In general, police officers are good people and want to do the right thing. They're just looking to keep the streets safe, and prevent drivers from violating traffic rules. I remember one time my sister was about eight months pregnant with two other kids in her vehicle. She had just had her appendix removed, which you can imagine was not the most comfortable during pregnancy and had limited mobility, although medically cleared to drive. She was driving home, and was pulled over because her registration was overdue. The police officer was very kind and offered to escort her to the nearest registry to renew it immediately rather than give her a large fine. He even offered to stand by the vehicle with the two little ones while she limped in to renew it to make it easier on her. He wasn't looking to "meet his ticket quota" as some people often say, or "have a power trip", he just wanted to make sure she was following the rules like everyone else and went out of his way to help her.

Sobriety Checkpoints

Another type of police pullover worth mentioning is called a sobriety check point. These happen quite frequently in the evening, through certain holidays, and on weekends sporadically. They are designed to cut down on impaired driving.

The police set up a designated area where they stop every vehicle, or randomly selected vehicles to check for impaired drivers. This happens in most states, with the exception of a few that don't allow it.

The officer will ask you where you are driving from and to, if you've been drinking, and the relationship to the passengers in the car. If they feel you are acting suspiciously or they smell alcohol they will most likely give you a breathalyzer test. Once you pass, they will send you along your way. They are nothing to be afraid of, and go really quickly.

I talked about some potentially scary police pullover situations throughout this chapter, but most driver's will never be put in that situation. In your lifetime as a driver, I am quite certain, you may only be pulled over a handful of times for minor things that don't require a very long stop, and certainly not a scary one. To this day, my mom has never been pulled over while driving, and she's been driving for close to 60 years! So it just goes to show you that if you are a safe driver that knows their traffic laws, you might never have to even go through a pull over process.

8

ACCIDENTS HAPPEN

"Remember that the worst accidents occur in the middle of the road"

— EUGENE MCCARTHY

Do you remember when you were first learning to ride a bike? It felt so awkward and uncomfortable at first. Once you got the hang of it with training wheels, you slowly built the confidence to take them off. Then you were ready to roll (pun intended), as you went from easy terrain like the driveway, to zooming around gravel roads with your friends and attempting jumps off ramps. I'm sure at some point in time during all those stages of learning, you fell off and got a few bumps and bruises. It happens even when you have the skills, follow the rules, and try to be safe. The same goes for driving a vehicle. As you gain your confidence and drive more often and in different situations, accidents may occur due to your fault, your inexperience to read other driver's well, or when another person on the road is driving very unsafely and you are in the wrong place at the wrong time.

No matter what kind of accident you may find yourself in, it's going to be something that you've never experienced before. You might feel fuzzy, light headed, sick with adrenaline, and unsure of what to do. Just remember to react quickly, and with common sense. Your reaction to the scene can make a big difference on someone's life and your future consequences. Let's discuss some possible scenarios of what can happen and the types of accidents you can encounter.

IF IT'S SURFACE DAMAGE, DON'T SWEAT IT

If you get into an accident and you are lucky enough to walk away with no injuries to anyone involved, you should consider yourself to be very fortunate. It's very easy for even the smallest accident to create injuries that are sometimes permanent.

It's still tough though, that first time you put a scratch or dent in your vehicle. Whether it's yours or your parents. Each situation has its own consequences.

I'm about to tell you a story that I haven't told a lot of people, and I still cringe thinking about it to this very day. The first time I got a new car, I was in University. I had saved up for a while, and my parents helped me out with the rest. The second week that I owned it I was in a parkade, and I had parked too close to a pole. As I was backing up and turning out of the parking spot the whole left side of the vehicle scraped along this yellow pole. I can still remember the awful crunching sound of the metal. When I saw my parents the next day, my dad was so upset, and he made the assumption that a yellow vehicle had scraped alongside of me in the parking lot, because I told him I didn't know what had happened. I was just so embarrassed that I had done something so stupid, that I couldn't bring myself to tell them that it was my fault. I still cringe thinking about the fact that I didn't tell them the truth. I will say that it made me a much more careful driver in parking lots and parkades, not to mention I never wanted to hear that crunching metal sound in an accident.

If you find yourself in the situation where are you put a dent scratch or dang in your vehicle, cut yourself some slack, at this point in time you're reducing the safety of your vehicle it's just aesthetics. It might feel like the worst thing in the world right now, but try and think of it in terms of how you feel about a year later. You probably won't even think about it. My dad used to also say "trying to keep a new car pristine is a fool's job". Part of me thinks that my dad always knew that it was my fault and then I scraped along a pole, and just went along with it to try and help me save face.

If an aesthetic scratch really bothers you on your vehicle, don't assume that you have to take it to a body shop to have it repaired. If it's serious enough you might have to, but with today's technology there's a lot of DIY fixes that you can do at home. One of my coworkers realized the other day that their blue truck had scratches along the front where it looks like another vehicle might have scraped along them, and they bought a matching colour off the Internet and you can't even tell the difference.

Parent Tip: If you make a little mistake and scratch your parent's vehicle, don't try and pretend you didn't know it happened or hope we don't notice. Just be honest, and try to offer a solution to help fix it. If one of my daughters scratched the car and tried to hide it, I probably wouldn't let her borrow it for a long time. If she was honest and open about what happened, I wouldn't be happy, but I would also be impressed by her honesty and commitment to correct it.

A FENDER BENDER AND ACCIDENTS WITH MINOR INJURIES AND DAMAGE

I have been in a few minor fender benders in my lifetime, most without injury. To be a little but more exact, I have been in four. I'll share my experiences so you can see how quickly a regular drive can turn into a bad day.

1. One time I was waiting in rush hour traffic at a stop light. The vehicle behind me wasn't paying attention and started accelerating before the light turned green and drove right into the back of my car. In this situation there wasn't a lot I could have done to prevent it. Fortunately because I left the correct amount of space in between me and the car in front of me, I wasn't pushed into him. This happens quite often when someone is rear ended in traffic, they are parked too close to the person in front of them so they are slammed into the back of their car, and now you are rear ending someone as well. In an accident like this, the person who hit you is at fault, and then you are at fault for the person you are pushed into. This might seem unfair, but it's your fault for not leaving enough space.

2. In the second accident I was in, I ran into a

cement block in a parkade. This was obviously my fault because I didn't see it and damaged my whole bumper and tire. I was coming down the ramp, and took the turn too sharply. I hit it pretty hard and actually broke my finger because it jammed into the dash of the vehicle at a weird angle. I also had minor whiplash which caused my neck to have quite a bit of pain for a few months.

3. The third accident was the one I mentioned earlier when I was driving home after a late night class and had someone turn into me. Luckily no one was hurt.

4. The last fender bender I was in I am still embarrassed about and it's 15 years later. I had rented a minivan because we wanted to test one out for a week or so before deciding to purchase one. I just didn't think a test drive through a dealership would give me a good enough experience, I wanted to drive it for longer. It was winter time, and our street always had deep ruts where cars could maneuver through the deep snow in the same tracks over and over. To back out of our driveway, you always had to give it a little extra gas to gain enough speed to launch the vehicle over the ruts, otherwise you would get stuck.

No one ever parked on the street, and I was used to my smaller SUV's length. On this particular day, I didn't take into consideration the length of the rented van, and I didn't look closely in my rear view mirror to see the car that was parked behind me from the family my neighbours were visiting. So I leaned on the gas a bit to get my rented minivan over the ruts and launched it right into the car behind me. I felt so bad, and it was such a stupid mistake on my part. But things like that happen and you have to know how to deal with the situation.

Steps Once an Accident Has Occurred

1. The first thing you do once an accident has happened is assess the surroundings and safety of your situation. If for example, you have hit wildlife as you came around the corner, you are sitting in a blind spot. You don't want to stay in a parked car in a blind spot, because another vehicle may come around the corner at a high speed and run right into you. If you are not in a safe place, or can safely exit the vehicle, try and move your vehicle to a safer spot.

2. If you are safe to get out of the vehicle, assess your own physical condition as well as the other vehicle's driver and passengers if you collided with another vehicle. You want to act quickly if someone's health has been affected to get proper medical help on site.

3. After you are sure that everyone is physically ok, assess the damage of the vehicles and what needs to happen to get everyone safely home. If the damage is minor and both vehicles are safe to drive, then move to the next step. If the damage is heavier, you will have to call police for help to come and assess the situation. If an accident creates enough damage, in most states you need what is called a damage sticker before a mechanic will do repairs. The purpose of a damage sticker is to ensure that you have reported the accident to the police and that you didn't participate in a hit and run. The police should be able to give you a damage sticker at the time of the accident. If the accident doesn't require police on site, and you are able to drive home, you will have to go to a police station and file a report and give you a damage sticker. You will then have to paste the damage sticker in your window until the vehicle is repaired to other police know that you have reported the accident. This helps them out because if they know a large accident was caused by a green car, and they see your green car with damage and no sticker, they will pull you over to find out more.

4. The next step is to exchange your insurance information. Prior to driving, make sure that you know how to contact your insurance company. We mentioned earlier that you would have to call the insurance company to make sure you were safe to drive under your parent's insurance, or if you needed your own. This is a great opportunity to also ask them what number you should call in case of emergency. Many insurance companies now Have their own app to speed of the declaration and documentation of an incident. Quite often the app has a quick button that will connect you with an insurance agent, or after hours give you instructions of what to do. In some of the insurance apps it gives you the opportunity to take photos of the damage, accident, and write a report of what your version of the events are. Just like your license and registration, make sure you know where your insurance card is at all times in a vehicle. Next you're going to exchange insurance information with the other driver, if your accident involved another vehicle. You will take their insurance information, and they will take yours. The reason you do this is because both of you were going to report the accident to the insurance company with the police report, and they will determine who is at fault and decide who will pay the deductible fees. When you sign up for insurance, they offer you something called a deductible rate. If you are found at fault in an accident, you must pay the deductible of your own Vehicle and the others in order to get them repaired. Sometimes companies will offer a deductible forgiveness policy of one time, then that means if you're only in one accident you won't be paying your deductible. Or they offer you a higher deductible for a lower monthly fee, but then if you're in an accident you'll have a higher deductible. Most commonly deductibles range from $250-$1000 depending on your age, driving record, policy, and company. If for whatever reason the other driver is resistant to exchange insurance information, make sure to take down their License plate at a bare minimum, and try to get their vehicle identification number from the police.

Alex is trying really hard to exchange insurance information with another driver but they are angry and refusing. Try not to escalate the situation and get the information you can.

5. The last step of the accident once everyone is safely on their way, is the phone call to your parents. Or if at any point in time during the accident steps you feel like you need more information or you are uncomfortable with how things are progressing, call your parents for help or advice. If they are close by, they will most likely want to come help you navigate through the situation. Make sure to be truthful with them about what happened, and keep communication open about the next steps.

Parent Tip: When you first call your parents to let them know that you have been in an accident, start with the following accident. "Mom or Dad, I am completely fine, and so is everyone else, but I have been in a car accident." That phone call is every parent's biggest fear when you start driving on your own, so leading the conversation by confirming that you are not hurt will be very appreciated.

In a more serious accident, you will follow the same steps above. There just may be the extra added factor of a more serious health emergency. If anyone is unsure of their health condition, an ambulance should be called right away. Call 911 and explain that a serious car accident has happened, and have them send police and an ambulance right away. They will ask you for more information, such as the location of the accident, how many people were involved, and the state of anybody in medical distress. They will stay on the phone with you until medical personnel and authorities arrive. The life-threatening situation they may walk you through certain steps to try and help the person in distress. Or if you were the one in distress to keep you calm. If being in a serious car accident and dealing with a medical emergency is something that makes you very uncomfortable or scared, a way to improve your confidence is to take a first aid course that will help you be more prepared in those emergency situations.

Alex isn't a medic, but this is the type of smiling face he would want to see if he was in need of medical attention. Remember if you were the one in need of help, you would want someone to get help immediately. Take medical distress seriously and act quickly.

YOUR LEGAL OBLIGATIONS AND RIGHTS AFTER AN ACCIDENT

After an accident, there are certain procedures that you have to follow to ensure everything is handled correctly.

First and foremost, never leave the scene of an accident without permission to do so. This applies to witnessing an accident as well. If you see the details of a collision and then keep on driving, no one may ever know, but it's not the legal or right thing to do. What if one of those driver's does a hit and run and someone is in serious medical distress. You could have been the one to call the ambulance or perhaps catch the license plate of the vehicle as it took off. If you keep driving you aren't there to tell authorities what happened to catch the person who took off illegally, or maybe the person in medical distress died because no one was there to help them. If you see an accident, stop. If you are involved in an accident, don't take off out of panic or fear. You will get caught and suffer huge consequences for your actions.

As we mentioned earlier, you are legally obligated to provide your name, contact info and insurance information to the other driver involved. You must also report the accident to the police and file a report. You can also only drive your vehicle away if it is road worthy. For example, if the bumper is dragging on the ground, or your turn signals don't work, you have to get it towed and cannot attempt to drive it to the repair shop yourself to save money.

It's your right as a driver to only speak with your insurance company and not the other driver's. You can contact your insurance company right away and give them the information of the other driver and they will handle everything between the two of you. Whether you are at fault or not, you can describe the accident to the best of your ability in the police report, but do not have to admit fault or sign anything until you speak to both your insurance company and lawyer. You do have to be honest and cooperative, but if things seem confusing to you, don't let the other driver or the police talk you into doing something that you are unclear about.

FOLLOWING UP WITH YOUR PARENTS

I mentioned that step 5 is calling your parents to get advice or let them know that you have been in an accident. This will probably be a shorter conversation, and I promise you there is a longer one coming later. It's our job as parents to worry about you, make sure you are safe, and help you understand your mistakes so that you can improve next time.

When you get home they are probably going to smother you. Alex remembers after his first accident feeling like he was being inspected and probed by aliens, as his parents swarmed him to make sure he was ok and to check him over for injuries they think he might not have been aware of. This might annoy you, but remember parents are doing it all out of love. The second we hear the words car accident in reference to one of our children, even if you are totally fine, we probably won't sleep for a week. So let us put our fears at ease and check you over and ask you a lot of questions, so just brace yourself for that impact.

Take the proper time to have a chat with your parents about everything that happened.

Now that Alex has his own teenager, he understands a bit better about what his parents went through after his first fender bender. He finds himself wanting to know all the details of what happened. What were the events leading up to the accident, who was involved, does he have a copy of the police report, did he contact his insurance yet? These are all things that as a parent we probably have experience with, and we want to help you as much as we can. And above all else, we want to make sure you are ok. Not just physically, but mentally as well. Getting into an accident can shatter your confidence as a driver and make you a little bit more shy or anxious on the road.

Don't be surprised if your parents are angry. Depending on their personality, their fear and stress may come out as frustration and anger as opposed to gentle concern. This doesn't mean that they aren't concerned, it's just their method of communicating to you how serious this is and hoping to prevent it from happening in the future.

Have open communication with your parents about how you are feeling. If you decide that you want to go back to driving under their supervision for a while, be honest about that. Do whatever you need to do to get comfortable behind the wheel and just make sure to be vocal about what you need.

Parent Tip: The first few days post-accident you and your parents are probably going to still be a bit shaken, and other than the police report and the insurance claim, not really thinking too much about the monetary impact of the accident. Once you've had a few days to think, approach your parents and discuss with them your plan, or ask to make a plan to cover the costs if there are any associated. This could be your deductible, tow truck fees, ambulance costs, and more. You may have to borrow money from them in which case come up with a plan to pay it back. As parents we expect that there are going to be costs associated with our kids driving, but we are also more appreciative and willing to help if our children don't take it for granted and offer to help.

Hopefully you are never put in the position where you are dealing with medical fallout from a tragic accident. I am happy to say I have been driving for many decades, and have not been in any major accidents other than my minor fender benders. The entire point of this book is to help get you out there safely so you hopefully never have to endure the pain of being responsible for taking a life, or injuring yourself and others. You do have to be prepared for any situation and understand that every time you get behind the wheel you are taking a small risk of getting into an accident. That being said, if you are very cautious and a safe, responsible driver, the odds are in your favor that you can stay safe and enjoy a lifetime of carefree driving.

9

COMMUNICATION WITH OTHER DRIVERS

O ut on the open road there is an entirely
different language between drivers. As a
passenger, you may have noticed your parents wave

sometimes, put their hazard lights on in certain situations, or noticed another vehicle flash their brights in your direction. These are all little signals that drivers use to communicate with each other because they can't verbally talk from one car to another or, in some cases, from a pedestrian to a vehicle.

Some communication between vehicles is meant to indicate what your movements while driving will be. For example, when you put your turn signal on, it indicates what direction you will be turning. This is communicating from your vehicle to the ones around you what you will be doing.

Some communication between vehicles is purely manners and etiquette. These aren't required but are really appreciated and keep everyone on the road civil and kind. For example, if you are trying to merge into traffic and someone slows down to let you in, giving them a quick wave says, "thank you." They didn't have to let you in, so waving shows your appreciation for their kindness. They had good manners and so did you.

The only way you can properly communicate with other vehicles is if you are constantly analyzing all the traffic and keeping your eyes moving at all times. This is another factor of focused driving that we have spoken about previously. Your surroundings can change in an instant, and you need to constantly be checking all of your mirrors and blind spots to make sure you know everything that's going on around you.

ANALYZING YOUR SURROUNDINGS

Like he's in a sci-fi movie, Alex is analyzing his surroundings as if he's never seen them before. Treat every moment in your car like it's a new scene that you've never seen before in a movie. You are constantly trying to figure out the moves of the other vehicles to anticipate your reaction. pretend they are aliens and that you are using non-verbal communication to be polite and not create confrontations.

Analyzing your surroundings isn't necessarily a natural skill for all drivers. One of my driving instructors did this great practice exercise where he would cover the rear view mirror and ask what color the car behind us was. The first time I was embarrassed and had no clue. The second time, I was mad at myself because I had been checking, but then started focusing on other things and stopped. The third time, I was prepared and got it right. He continued to do it sporadically throughout all of our lessons, and eventually it just became a habit.

This same driving instructor would always ask after I went through a controlled intersection if it was a "good green light" or a "bad green light." He was referring to the walk light that coincided with the timing of the light. If the pedestrian light was still telling pedestrians to go ahead and walk, that meant there was a lot of time, and it was a "good green light." If the hand was flashing and telling pedestrians to wait, then it was considered a "bad green light," because the light would turn to yellow soon. It was also a great exercise to practice analyzing my surroundings and pay attention to small details.

It probably looks like your parents are just staring forward when they are driving, and you don't realize how much information they are actually taking in at every moment. As a good exercise, ask a more experienced driver to take you out and describe to you what they are looking at and noticing at every moment. With experience, you would be able to close your eyes (which you would never do while driving) and describe all the vehicles around you, any pedestrians nearby, street signs, and possible upcoming dangers.

Upcoming Dangers

What do I mean when I say upcoming dangers? As you are scanning, you will see things coming up that may create the need for you to respond. Chances are you won't, but you have to be aware of possibilities. Here are some scenarios as examples:

Scenario 1:

You are driving in rush hour traffic, and you notice that one lane seems to be a lot slower. As you get closer, you can see up ahead that a vehicle has stalled and is blocking a lane of traffic. By analyzing and noticing that a lane of traffic was moving slower, it allowed you to safely merge away from the slow lane and avoid a potential accident with the stalled vehicle and other's trying to get around it.

Scenario 2:

You are driving through a neighbourhood and notice a vehicle coming up that will be turning left, which will cause them to drive out in front of you. You are close enough that they should wait until after you pass, but you notice they are turned the other way and not paying attention that you are approaching. You start to slow your pace in anticipation. Sure enough they are only watching the traffic coming towards you, and as a vehicle passes, they pull out right in front of you. You are able to react and make a hard stop to avoid a collision. Even though it would have been their fault, you would have hit the driver's side at full speed and possibly really injured them. By being such a proactive driver, you may have just saved their life.

Scenario 3:

Shortly after you avoid a collision with that car turning left, you are shaken but still driving along in the same neighbourhood. You take notice of some kids playing up ahead in their driveway. You slow your pace just in case. One of the kids sees their friend across the street and runs out right in front of you towards them. You anticipated that this scenario could happen so you are going at a slow enough pace with plenty of time to stop.

Hopefully you are starting to get the picture of the type of things that can come up really quickly and the reason why you have to constantly scan your surroundings to keep everyone safe. The hope is that the other drivers are also doing the same things, but they aren't always so don't rely on their behavior to keep your car safe.

When it comes to other drivers, you can sometimes judge a book by its cover a little bit. The same as people giving you a little bit more patience and space because of your new driver sign, you might want to steer clear of drivers with cars in rough shape. For example, if you are pulling into a parking spot and you notice that the vehicle next to you has a bunch of scrapes and small dents, you might want to find a new parking place.

You also want to drive a little differently around certain types of vehicles. Both semi-trucks and motorcycles are good examples. Semi trucks deserve extra attention because they have larger blind spots, they maneuver differently, and they are slower to react due to their size. They usually give themselves a lot more time to slow down and stop at lights, and it drives me crazy when I see vehicles whip around them and slide in front to get ahead. They give themselves extra space and time, and drivers are not always that polite about it. For your safety, give semi trucks lots of space.

Pedestrian

Make sure to take extra caution when dealing with pedestrians. You want to assume that pedestrians are going to be extra careful because they're the ones that don't have protection against vehicles, but you also don't want to be responsible for injuring a pedestrian if they aren't paying attention. When you're at a red or green light, we talk about analyzing the situation at all times. So make sure that you take note of how many pedestrians there are, how many are crossing, and how many are close by coming up the street that may try and run across at the last minute. Try to make eye contact with pedestrians if they are waiting for you to stop to cross the street. Smile and wave and let them know that you see them and that you are not in danger. Being polite to pedestrians is important because I'm sure you are a pedestrian a lot of the time too. Again it's just about having good manners.

Alex is out for a walk as a pedestrian. Since he is quite often a pedestrian, he knows that you can get distracted and forget to watch for vehicles. As a driver he pays extra attention to pedestrians to make sure they are safe.

DRIVERS ETIQUETTE IN A FEW EASY STEPS

Alex is waving to a driver behind him to thank him for letting him merge in. Good manners and etiquette go a long way on the road. It can be tough to remember to be friendly and kind when you are so focused on keeping your driving safe, so here are 5 easy points to remember.

1. Good etiquette starts with keeping your distance. Always stay back from another car when following them. Even if you are in a rush, and they are driving under the speed limit, don't ride their bumper in an attempt to speed them up. The rule of thumb in normal driving conditions is "three seconds plus." When the vehicle in front of you passes something stationary on the side of the road such as a building, begin counting. You reach that same building no sooner than three seconds. When your visibility is poor, make that distance even bigger.

2. Do not get distracted with your phone or take your eyes off the road. This applies at traffic lights too. Nothing makes me more irritable than when I see a vehicle swerving and driving erratically and I can see that they are texting. It's extremely dangerous and rude that they don't have the respect for other driver's lives.

3. Communicate accurately and timely signals with lights and gestures. Don't be that person that is turning on their signal light as they are turning. Make sure to do it 10 seconds before so the people behind you know that you will be slowing down.

4. Be aware of other cars blind spots, and try not to stay in them. It's not a safe place to be for you, and unsafe for the other driver as well. By staying in their blind spot, they have to constantly monitor where you are, and it might distract them from other things.

5. Give off a calm and confident vibe with small and smooth movements of your vehicle. Anxious driver's can cause accidents by hesitating or making quick jerking motions. An example would be when someone is entering a freeway from a merge lane. Rather than speeding up to match the speed of the other vehicles and merging safely, they panic and slam on their breaks putting vehicles behind them at risk.

Good etiquette also comes from cultural norms in your area. When I lived in a smaller, rural town, it was very common to vehicles to wave at each other as they drove by. It was rude if you didn't. It took me a long time when I moved to a bigger city to realize that it was weird for the driver's there. Ask your parents about manners and etiquette specific to your area.

DEFENSIVE AND AGGRESSIVE DRIVING

Here's Alex driving both defensively and aggressively. Whose car would you want to be in? Also who would you want to be on the road with?

Defensive driving is a much safer way to be. Defensive driving is everything we have talked about in the book. It's analyzing your surroundings, steering clear of trouble, being cautious, and following the rules. You communicate well to other drivers and look out for everyone's best interests on the road.

An aggressive driver is more prone to causing and being in accidents. They drive more emotionally, and often react without thinking. They tailgate, yell, speed, and weave in and out of traffic. They typically are the type of driver that a defensive driver will actively avoid.

I'm not going to pretend that you are either completely one or the other. Every once in a while, your emotions might get the best of you, or you might speed up a little bit. Try to acknowledge or notice when you are driving aggressively and switch up your behaviour before you get hurt.

Parent Tip: Driver's that are new and seem to be aggressive are terrifying to parents. My daughter was once on her way home from school with one of her friends driving, and she called me to ask something. I could hear her friend swearing at other people in the background and the engine revving as she waited at a light. I didn't say anything at the time, but as soon as my daughter was home I told her she wasn't allowed in that friend's vehicle anymore. Being an aggressive driver is not cool and has no benefit.

10

TIPS TO MAKE YOU LOOK LIKE A CAR EXPERT (PLUS THE 3 TIPS I PROMISED)

There's certain car knowledge that most people don't expect you to know for a long time. So if you show up on day one of driving with this level of knowledge, you're going to look like an expert and really impress your friends and parents. These tips are my extra gift to you for taking the time to read this book and make yourself into a safer and more confident driver.

CAR EXPERT TIP 1: BREAKING IN A VEHICLE

If you bought yourself a new car, first of all I will say congratulations! That is an exciting day, and one you'll probably remember forever. Make sure to get a picture of you in your first car, you'll probably look back on it 50 years from now fondly.

What your dealer doesn't tell you is that for the first thousand miles of your new vehicle, you have to drive it differently than you will in the future. You have to be very gentle with it to break in the mechanical parts and to avoid future expenses down the road. Use the following tips to break it in properly:

- Do not use cruise control
- Don't excessively rev the engine
- Check your oils and other fluids more regularly than you normally would, just to ensure that nothing is leaking and that nothing is running without fluid
- Try not to perform hard stops while driving, unless it's an emergency for safety

- Always make sure the gas tank is never near empty
- Don't open the throttle up and go full speed
- Very your RPM in the middle range while driving
- Avoid having your vehicle towed at all costs

CAR EXPERT TIP 2: GET THE MOST OUT OF YOUR TIRES

We have talked a lot about your tires and how important proper maintenance is to your safety. Another thing to think about is the cost of your tires. They are not cheap, and you want to get the most out of them. Here is a list of tips to make sure you can keep them going safely for as long as you can:

- Keep the total weight of your vehicle light. Don't overload and carry around extra items
- Defensive driving such as giving yourself plenty of time to slow down as opposed to hard stops will prevent excessive wearing
- Don't underinflate them.
- Rotate them every six months
- Check your alignment regularly

There are some things that you can't control such as the weather you drive in which some might be harder on tires than others. You also can't control how much city vs. highway driving you do. Driving in the city is harder on tires because it requires more stopping and starting and creates more wear.

When it comes time to buy new tires, many driver's shy away from retreaded ones. Retreaded tires have been given a bad reputation as unsafe or poorer quality, but they are legal for a reason. They are safe, more budget friendly, and better for the environment than new tires. So, in my opinion and many others, they are a great option. You will look very smart with that tip because not a lot of people are even aware of retreaded tires.

CAR EXPERT TIP 3: BUYING A USED CAR LIKE A PRO

When you are ready to buy your own vehicle, a used car is a great option! It opens up more options to you for variety, because there is a range of prices, inventory, and sources to choose from. I want to help you get the most out of buying a used car because it can sometimes be a tricky process. Unfortunately there's a reason why there's the old stereotype of a "used car salesmen." It can be a landmine of opportunities for someone to take advantage of you. That's not to say that all dealerships are like this or people in general. Especially not in today's world where there's so much information at your fingertips. But you just want to know the right questions to ask, and what to look for. So, here are seven tips to finding your own vehicle:

1. Decide what your budget is and do your research. When you get into an environment where there are a lot of options and a lot of different budgets, it can be very easy to get swayed into something more expensive. Set your budget based on the price of the vehicle, your insurance, your registration, possible maintenance and monthly gas.

2. Once you have an idea of what kind of vehicle you were looking for, do some research online and see what you should be paying for that vehicle. Take into account the year, the mileage, the options, and the way the vehicle was maintained.

3. Consider all your financing options. You may have been saving up which is great. If not you can ask your parents for a loan, and or talk to potential lenders about their options and rates. You may have to get your parents to cosign a loan, but it shows them how serious you are about being fiscally responsible.

4. Once you decide on a car, run a history report on it. There are a few options for this, including Carfax, vincheck, and vehicle history. You'll get a report of everything the vehicle has gone through including accidents or troubles. Be on the lookout for:

a. Major accidents

b. mileage rollback

c. multiple owners

d. structural damage

e. vehicle service history

5. Take the vehicle for a test drive. Bring your parent or another more experienced driver along who will be able to spot things that you may not see. If possible try and test the car in a variety of conditions. This means taking it on different types of roads and at different speeds.

6. Make sure to get the vehicle inspected. Before you give any money to the seller, ask to have the vehicle inspected by your own mechanic. A seller may have an inspection report, but you never know who it's done by. It could've been performed by their best friend and not have all the information that you need. The seller should have no issue with it if the vehicle is in good condition.

Have the mindset that you can walk away from a deal at any point in time. If something doesn't feel right, no matter how good the deal is, be prepared to shop around. A great example of this is a friend of mine who is about to buy a truck off of a classified ad. The owner seemed very trustworthy, and the vehicle seemed in great shape. They were about to pay for an inspection, when the owner made a comment that made them walk away. The owner told him that the vehicle was so durable, he had never changed the oil. Never changed the oil?! The vehicle had 60,000 miles on it. My friend loved that truck but walked away and never looked back.

The amount of information you can access online in today's world for buying vehicles is astounding. There are even a variety of platforms that you can use online that are specific only to purchasing vehicles and lay out the information very clearly to a first time buyer. Here are few of the top sites online today:

- **AutoTempest:** This website is kind of like the kayak or expedia for cars. It displays for you information from several different websites all at once to make your decision making process easy. You can also search for information and reviews on any make and model, and get quotes on new cars in your area.
- **Cars.com:** The inventory on cars.com is unrivaled by any of its competitors. They have such a broad network of affiliates, it's the most widely used site and has the most to choose from.

- **Autobytel:** Autobytel has many cool features that makes buying a vehicle exciting. They have their widely popular top 10 lists in every category you can think of. They also have a tool that helps you decide what vehicle is right for you based on a series of questions. That one is fun to do even if you're not purchasing a vehicle. They are one of the largest search engines for finding both new and used vehicles. They also have a ton of information regarding car reviews and financing.

- **eBay Motors:** What made eBay famous was its bidding system and it works for cars too! Do your research first and then try to get a deal on a local purchase.

- **Facebook Marketplace and Craigslist** - What doesn't Facebook do nowadays? If you are looking to purchase locally it's a great option with usually a lot of inventory and high turnover. You can keep checking daily to see what new vehicles are added. With both options, you can make a short list and then set out to test drive the vehicles in a short time frame. It's less stressful and you don't have to worry about what you are buying because you can see it. Don't go alone to test drive vehicles. Take someone with you for safety as you don't know who you are meeting on the other end of the sale.

Use these platforms and your own research to narrow down exactly what you are looking for. Involve your parents in the process because they might have some insights and wisdom that you might not think of on your own. Plus it will be fun and exciting for them to be a part of the process too.

CONCLUSION

As I said in the beginning of the book, getting your license is one of the most exciting things that'll happen to you. I've always equated having my license with freedom.

A lot of the book probably got a little bit heavy, and I hope it was nothing that intimidated you or made you feel scared about driving. Operating a vehicle is very serious. It's a large heavy machine that can go very fast, and things can go wrong very quickly. The only reason we discuss all the possibilities is to make sure that you're really confident and prepared for any situations that arise.

As a parent, I always wanted to make sure my girls were prepared for anything. They were always the ones that knew how to use jumper cables if someone needed a boost, they've always been able to change their own tires, and they've always known the questions to ask when they take their vehicle into a dealership. At this point in time, thankfully neither have gotten into any major accidents and, other than a few parking lot scrapes, they haven't really had to deal with insurance either. But, I want to make sure that I remind them of the steps and ways that they need to deal with things if they arise.

That's what this book is for, not to scare you or concern you about all the situations that might happen. It's to prepare you in case they do. Use it as a refresher every couple years. Chances are you might not remember the steps of what to do when you're in an accident. It's been so long since I've had an accident, I had to do a little research to remember exactly what the steps are for dealing with an insurance company. I didn't even have the app downloaded and there's to say. But now I've given myself a refresher, and I feel prepared for anything.

As you read this book, things come up that you may not have realized. Make sure to have that open communication and conversations with your parents. Depending on where you live, rules and regulations might vary slightly from things I've talked about in the book. And there might be special considerations for areas that you love that I didn't cover. So talk to them about things that come up along as you read. Take notes, be that good student that you were in the beginning when you study for your driver's license, and ask the questions after you're done reading.

Growing up, my mom had this great saying, always keep your wits about you. It was one of those things that she said so often I kind of stopped listening after a while. But then, as I became a parent and as I started to teach my daughters how to drive, I realized how relevant it was. It really does encompass all the lessons that we've learned.

You can't keep your wits about you if you're intoxicated with drugs or alcohol, speeding, stressed, or in and in some other emotional state that you shouldn't be driving. So, you definitely shouldn't drive if any of those things are going to affect you. You can keep your wits about you if you're calm, focused, clear headed, and driving safely. All these things add up to keeping you safe on the road. If, at any point in time, one of these things falters or changes, that's when it puts you and other drivers in danger. So, it might seem like you're constantly over analyzing or playing it too safe or putting too much work into keeping the maintenance of your vehicle. But the truth is that driving is a privilege and although it is probably one of the most fun things in the world, it's also one of the leading causes of death and accidents in the US as well. So make sure to always follow your gut, be safe, gain experience, and, most of all, keep your wits about you.

REFERENCES

All photos sourced from pixabay.com

"6 Things You Need to Know about Tire Pressure." *Nonda*, 1 Dec. 2020, www.nonda.co/blogs/news/6-things-you-need-to-know-about-tire-pressure. Accessed 12 Aug. 2021.

"Anti-Lock Braking System: MyCarDoesWhat.org." *My Car Does What*, 2015, mycardoeswhat.org/safety-features/anti-lock-braking-system/.

"Dodge Journey Problems and Complaints - 12 Issues." *RepairPal.com*, repairpal.com/problems/dodge/journey. Accessed 17 Aug. 2021.

"FAQs about Your Car's Fuel and Air Filters | Firestone Complete Auto Care."

Www.firestonecompleteautocare.com, 22 Aug. 2016, www. firestonecompleteautocare.com/blog/maintenance/ faqs-about-your-cars-cabin-fuel-and-air-filters/. Accessed 10 Aug. 2021.

"Four Reasons Your ABS Light Is On." *Christian Brothers Automotive,* 19 June 2019, www.cbac.com/media-center/blog/2019/june/four-reasons-your-abs-light-is-on/. Accessed 10 Aug. 2021.

"Know Someone Learning to Drive? We're Here to Help!" *Driver's Ed Guru,* driversedguru.com/. Accessed 2 Aug. 2021.

Liquori, Thomas. "Everything You Need to Know about Engine Performance | Rislone USA." *Rislone.com,* 1 Nov. 2019, rislone.com/engine/everything-you-need-to-know-about-engine-performance/. Accessed 12 Aug. 2021.

Nikola Djurkovic. "24 Texting and Driving Statistics (2019 Update)." *Carsurance,* carsurance, 4 June 2019, carsurance.net/blog/texting-and-driving-statistics/.

"Speeding." *Injury Facts,* injuryfacts.nsc.org/motor-vehicle/motor-vehicle-safety-issues/speeding/.

Made in United States
Orlando, FL
17 December 2021